How to
Impress Anybody
About Anything

How to Impress Anybody About Anything

*Sound Smarter Than You Are
About Everything From
Aerodynamics to Zen Buddhism*

**Leslie Hamilton
Brandon Toropov**

A Citadel Press Book
Published by Carol Publishing Group

A Citadel Press Book
Published by Carol Publishing Group
Citadel Press is a registered trademark of Carol Communications, Inc.

Editorial, sales and distribution, rights and permissions inquiries should be
addressed to Carol Publishing Group, 120 Enterprise Avenue, Secaucus, N.J.
07094.

In Canada: Canadian Manda Group, One Atlantic Avenue, Suite 105, Toronto,
Ontario M6K 3E7

Carol Publishing Group books may be purchased in bulk at special discounts
for sales promotion, fundraising, or educational purposes. Special editions can
be created to specifications. For details, contact Special Sales Department,
Carol Publishing Group, 120 Enterprise Avenue, Secaucus, N.J. 07094.

Manufactured in the United States of America
10 9 8 7 6 5 4 3 2 1

Library of Congress Cataloging-in-Publication Data

Hamilton, Leslie.
    How to impress anybody about anything : sound smarter than you are
about everything from aerodynamics to Zen Buddhism / Leslie
Hamilton, Brandon Toropov.
        p. cm.
    "A Citadel Press Book."
    ISBN 0–8065–1985–1
    1. Curiosities and wonders. I. Toropov, Brandon. II. Title.
AG243.H24   1998
031.02—dc21
                                                                98–5732
                                                                CIP

Contents

Acknowledgments

Leslie's thanks go out to...

Jim, my editor and phone friend, for having so much patience with me and for making me feel special when I needed it. The town of Ipswich, the hippest town on this coast at least. To the Ipswich Public Library, may it keep ever growing. To Elizabeth and Kim at Fun Among Us for all the fun I had among them. The women of Sip and Sew; the wisest women I've ever met. Let them forever eat cake. The gang at the Video Barn for believing in me first. To William Feldeman, the family jeweler. To Squire Roland A. Dudney, O.B.E. of her Majesty's Horse Guardsmen, Order of the Garter and all around great guy. And Mandy Hogan, equestrian extraodinaire and fellow Thelwell fan. To Jim "Gillie" Gilford for taking the time to teach a girl about cigars. I think of you whenever I indulge. To Glenny for the computer power. To Mark for the sage advice, a sensitive man who knows of what he speaks—thanks for the perspective. To Andrew Cote, my first baby. To my mom, the really smart one in the family, and Francis for the flowers and the "would I's!" And to Meghan, for all the support as always; to Emma for making me laugh and all the back rubs; to Cassie for chasing the seagulls away, all the cuddles, and keeping her clothes on, for the most part; Mommy loves you three more than you will ever know.

Finally to Bob, who knows me like no other and still loves me. Thanks for every gesture, every kiss and for doing all the math. Could a woman have a better husband? Well they can't have mine. I love you forever.

Brandon's thanks go to:
My wife, Mary, Jim Ellison, Ann Boder, Glenn KnicKrehm, Mark Waldstein, Henry Tragert, and Mary Tragert. And everyone Leslie thanked, especially the librarians; whose patience never ceases to amaze me.

Introduction

Will this book reveal all the mysteries of existence to you? Will it inspire you to superhuman feats of intellectual achievement? Will it help turn you into another Socrates, William Shakespeare, Lao Tzu, or Stephen Hawking? Or will it merely pass along a few choice nuggets to dispense as the need arises at the next Trivial Pursuit party? Will it help you sound good for a few moments at a time, perhaps on a popular game show that awards successful contestants thousands of dollars in cash and prizes? Will it reveal some shrewd strategies for holding your own for a glorious minute or two during conversations in which you might otherwise be out of your depth?

The answer, as it so often does, lies somewhere between the two. *How to Impress Anybody About Anything* provides you with the straight scoop on all kinds of interesting and potentially daunting topics, from aerodynamics to Zen Buddhism. It offers concise, on-the-level summaries of a dizzying variety of subjects—enough information to get you through a cocktail party encounter, but also enough to spark your interest, encourage more learning from other sources, and, who knows, perhaps propel you toward that Nobel Prize you always knew was just within reach, if only you had the right jumping-off point.

You will find, near the end of each section, some advice on *extricating* yourself from the discussion in question. This advice came in quite handy, especially if you find yourself trapped in a conversation about, say, the Big Bang with someone who turns out to be both (a) boorish and (b) incredibly well informed. The idea here is not to sound smarter than you are because you want people to think you're an expert in a given field, but to sound smarter than you are because it's often an enjoyable way to get an otherwise dormant conversation moving in a pleasant direction. I'm certainly not advocating intellectual deception here; instead, I'm advocating the process of projecting a well-informed persona in a given area for long enough to get the other person talking. To me, that's an excellent strategy for *learning* more about the topic you've chosen. After all, no one is an expert on *everything*.

Consider William F. Buckley, who once related the story of how, immediately before a broadcast of his program *Firing Line,* the guest for the hour, then-Senator Albert Gore, who was to discuss the Tennessee Valley Authority, leaned forward and whispered, "Mr. Buckley, I want you to know something—I know more about the Tennessee Valley Authority than you do." Buckley smiled and continued the interview normally.

The point to bear in mind? Even a public figure who boasts a persona associated with unyielding intellectual supremacy—and, yes, the barest hint of arrogance now and then—has his blind spots. And even with those blind spots a constructive, enlightening exchange of views is possible. So don't give up too easily. Try to keep your conversational partner engaged. Get that give-and-take going. Then, if you find yourself trapped in a world you did not create, follow the advice that appears near the end of each section and hightail it to another, safer subject.

Remember: In most cases, you'll be looking not to score points off your conversational partner but to open up new possibilities for informed discussion. Who *knows* what you'll learn after that? It's hard to believe now, in this wired, supercharged, video-driven age, but whole evenings used to be spent in the pursuit of intelligent conversation. The aim of those gatherings wasn't for one participant to demonstrate his or her superiority over the rest of the pack, but rather for the group as a whole to share feelings of discovery and wonder about the world in which they lived.

Consider this book to be the starting point, not the ending point, in your quest to learn what you can about the many subjects discussed here. Consider it an invaluable tool for those occasions when you know you may have to fake your way through a party full of bigtime movers and shakers. Consider it a good way to have some actual fun while reading about a lot of important stuff you probably should have been paying more attention to while you were in school. Most of all, consider *How to Impress Anybody About Anything* your excuse to browse freely. Consider us your guides as you skip lightly around the weighty topics discussed within these covers—for the best of all possible reasons, because you want to, not because you have to. That's the reason we wrote the book—because it was fun to do so. And let us take this opportunity to assure you that we're *not* experts in all the subjects discussed in these pages—though we are ready, willing, and eager to do research on topics that interest us. Thankfully, all the topics in this book fall into that category. We hope they do the same for you.

Enjoy!

Leslie Hamilton and Brandon Toropov

How to
Impress Anybody
About Anything

Truth means the fulfillment of our self; and moral law means following the law of our being. Truth is the beginning and end, the substance of natural existence. Without truth there is no material existence. It is for this reason that the moral man values truth. Thus, absolute truth is indestructible; being indestructible, it is eternal. Being eternal, it is self-existent. Being self-existent, it is infinite. Being infinite, it is vast and deep.... Thus Confucius went on to say: "Love of knowledge is akin to wisdom."

—TZE-SZE (CHINESE PHILOSOPHER AND GRANDSON OF CONFUCIUS)

The pleasure and delight of knowledge and learning, it far surpasseth all other in nature.... We see in all other pleasures there is satiety, and after they are used their verdure departeth; which showeth well they be but the deceits of pleasures, and not pleasure; and that it was the novelty that pleasured, not the quality.

—FRANCIS BACON

We hold these truths to be sacred and undeniable... That Almighty God hath created the mind free;—that all attempts to influence it by temporal punishments, or burdens or by civil incapacitations, tend only to beget habits of hypocrisy and meanness.... that truth is great and will prevail if left to herself; that she is the proper and sufficient antagonist to error, and has nothing to fear from the conflict unless by human interposition disarmed of her natural weapons, free argument and debate, errors ceasing to be dangerous when it is permitted freely to contradict them.

—FROM THOMAS JEFFERSON'S ORIGINAL DRAFT
OF THE DECLARATION OF INDEPENDENCE

HOW TO IMPRESS ANYBODY ABOUT

Aerodynamics and Aviation

Ever been eight miles high? If you said yes, odds are you were either smoking something you shouldn't have been, or were riding in a vehicle that took advantage of the principles of aerodynamics. Here's a quick rundown on how you pulled it off.

The Straight Scoop

Aerodynamics is a branch of physics concerned with the study of forces exerted by rushing air or other moving fluids. It is essential to the development of technology that must move through air (such as aircraft, missiles, and rockets). Aviation has to do with flight itself, generally in heavier-than-air craft.

The practical goal of those who are interested in aerodynamics is usually to employ existing knowledge to develop designs that will allow a moving body to take advantage of the greatest possible efficiency while moving through Earth's atmosphere. In order to gain this efficiency, designers usually incorporate a streamlined flow that generates the least possible turbulence by the moving object.

When an airplane flies through the air, there are four main forces acting on it. One is lift, courtesy of the Bernoulli principle, which holds that air passing above the specially shaped wing will gain speed thus reducing pressure below that of the surrounding atmosphere. The second force is the plane's own weight. (When a plane is flying level, the force of the lift and the weight are the same.)

The third force is drag, which pulls the airplane backward and must be overcome by the power of the engine. That brings us to the fourth force: thrust, caused by the rapid backward acceleration of the air stream, either as the result of propellors or the exhaust of a jet engine, which decreases the pressure in front of the plane.

What's that? You say that the bit about the Bernoulli principle went by you a little too fast? This contribution to human knowledge, which, among other things, made in-flight meals possible, arose from the work of the eighteenth-century scientist Daniel Bernoulli, who proposed that the speed of a fluid (yes, air counts as a fluid) is inversely related to its pressure. In other words, the faster the air goes, the lower the air pressure. Pressure differences on the top and bottom surfaces of an airfoil provide lift—but only because the airfoil (broadly curved in the front, flat on the bottom, and pointed at the back) is shaped in such a way as to speed up the air that passes above it. The result? The differing air pressures above and below the wing yield a distinct upward force.

Airplanes, which must employ a tail with horizontal and vertical elements to maintain stability, are designed to perform at certain speeds. The final shape of an aircraft is a product of the speed at which it is meant to travel.

What You Can Say

"The faster a plane has to go, the more streamlined it needs to be." (This explains the severe needlenose look of supersonic aircraft.) Fighter pilots have often been heard to remark of a plane that is not streamlined, "It has all the glide of a set of car keys."

"Supersonic planes can be pretty cool—they may redesign themselves in mid-flight!" (Some planes designed to travel faster than the speed of sound feature swing wings. When these planes are flying at low speeds the wings are extended and when they're flying at high speeds the wings are pulled back.)

"The Wright brothers are famous for conducting the first powered, controlled, and piloted flight—but an unmanned ninety-second flight took place seven years earlier." (Thanks to the work of Samuel

Langley, a pioneering U.S. scientist, whose craft *Model No. 5* flew over the Potomac River in 1896.)

When You Want to Change the Subject...

You might point out that the Wright brothers had rather limited choices when it came to in-flight movies. From that point, you can guide the discussion toward entertainment—or the lack thereof—on modern commercial flights. Or you point out how major airlines tried, and failed, to censor the scenes in *Rain Man* that mentioned all those plane crashes.

Maybe it's a movie you shouldn't see while you're tens of thousands of feet above the ground, after all.

Words to the Wise

Some people are extremely skittish about air travel. Respect, and do not belittle, their feelings—particularly if they've been involved in some hair-raising plunge that you haven't. Talking blithely about how safe flying is to someone who's felt a craft start to plummet isn't likely to endear you.

American History

American history is a rich, many-layered topic that admits many complex views and is capable of inspiring intense disagreements What follows is only a thumbnail sketch of principal events.

The Straight Scoop

No account of American history would be complete without acknowledging the horrific abuses sustained by Native American peoples as the process of "settling" the United States unfolded and the injustices suffered by blacks at the hands of slaveowners. Both of these epic human catastrophes were well under way by the time European residents of the thirteen individual colonies began to chafe under English authority in the late eighteenth century.

After the American victory over the British in the Revolutionary War (1775–1783) resulted in political independence, a movement arose to revise the (awkward) confederation under which the former colonies had joined together. The new arrangement: a constitution (1787; *see separate entry:* "The U.S. Constitution") that mandated a federal government based on the idea of checks and balances. Military hero George Washington, who had orchestrated the victory over the British, was elected the country's first president.

The nation grew westward quickly; the Louisiana Purchase (1803) was the largest and most dramatic of these expansions, roughly doubling the size of the young country. The War of 1812—rooted in trade-related disputes with Great Britain and a belief that the English had gone beyond the pale by supporting Indian tribes—led to renewed conflict. Although several U.S. military victories boosted feelings of patriotism and confidence among Americans, the conflict was inconclusive. The annexation of Texas (1845) resulted in another huge geographical expansion; it also led to a war with Mexico that the Americans won easily (1848). However, the question of Texas's status served as the latest flashpoint in a series of domestic political conflicts that underscored deep American divisions over the issue of slavery; disputes over the "free" or "slave" orientation of new states resulted in bitter regional conflicts and ever more serious political instability. Upon the election of Abraham Lincoln in 1860, Southern states began to turn talk of secession into action—and, eventually, into the Confederate States of America. Full-blown civil war erupted in 1861. (*See separate entry:* "The Civil War.") The extraordinarily bloody conflict ground on until 1865, when Union forces prevailed over the Confederacy. The Civil War was followed by the so-called Reconstruction period, a tumultuous phase marked by military occupation of the devastated Southern states, accusations of corruption and incompetence in new state governments, and, eventually, federal ambivalence over the abuse of blacks whose civil rights had supposedly been guaranteed by new constitutional amendments.

Extraordinary economic growth and industrial development also followed the Civil War; a major milestone in the nation's growth was the completion of the transcontinental railroad in 1869. War with Spain (1898) led to further acquisition of territories by the United States; Hawaii was annexed in the same year. The United States was a late (1917) entrant into World War I; a period of robust economic growth followed in the 1920s but was cut short by the disastrous stock market crash of 1929, the first of a series of shocks that led to the prolonged, catastrophic economic freefall known as the Great Depression. The election of Franklin D. Roosevelt in 1933, which led to the adoption of many elements of his New Deal economic program, brought renewed stability, purpose, and hope to a nation that had been on the brink of social and economic collapse. (However, the specific elements of Roosevelt's early economic policies were probably not as great a success as the overall confidence his leadership inspired in a nation that had been severely traumatized by economic reversals.)

American entry into World War II followed the Japanese attack on Pearl Harbor (1941); after Allied victory over the Axis powers (1945), there followed a period of enhanced American influence as a leader of Western (non-Communist) countries. Bitter rivalry with Communist nations marked the Cold War period (*see separate entry:* "The Cold War"), during which American forces were embroiled in bloody conflicts in Korea (1950–1953) and Vietnam (early 1960s to mid-1970s). To the degree that the phrase Cold War describes the period of tension and worldwide competition for influence between the United States and the Soviet Union, that period is usually regarded as ending in 1989, when the Soviet empire showed signs of fatal disarray and the idea of Soviet satellite countries in Europe began to become archaic. The United States thus emerged as the single superpower, a role with duties that have proved difficult to define precisely in the last decade of the twentieth century despite the country's success as a leader of the coalition arrayed against Iraq during the Gulf War (1991). In recent years, concerns over economic and environmental issues have played leading roles in American social and political affairs.

What You Can Say

The strategy here is pretty simple—pick a shrewd observation about a particular period of American history from the list below, deliver it with charm and confidence, and then wait for your conversational partner to pick up the ball and run with it. Herewith, a few reliable *bons mots* about the history of this nation of ours.

"Of course, if Benedict Arnold had died at Saratoga, he would have gone down in history as one of the heroes of the Revolutionary War." (Arnold's treason took place *after* his undeniably heroic service at, among other battles, Saratoga [1777]. Many believe that Arnold's betrayal of the American cause in 1780 arose from a feeling of having been less than adequately recognized for his past heroism on the battlefield. After fleeing to the British side when his plot to betray West Point to them was discovered, Arnold led several brutal British attacks on American positions in Virginia and Connecticut.)

"Lots of people confuse the Missouri Compromise with the Compromise of 1850." (Not you, though. You know that the Missouri Compromise was hammered out between 1819 and 1821, and resulted in Missouri's admission as a slave state and Maine's admission as a free state, with the prohibition of slavery in the territories that later became Kansas and Nebraska. What the Missouri Compromise really did was buy some time before the Union fell apart over the slavery issue. The Compromise of 1850 allowed California to enter the Union as a free state, and left the question of slavery in some new territories to be determined by the residents there. It, too, was virtually impossible to hammer out, and what it really accomplished was to buy a little *more* time before the Union fell apart over the slavery issue.)

"Well, depending on the federal government to spearhead social change has always been a risky proposition. *Plessy v. Ferguson* stood as the law of the land for more than half a century." (This 1898 Supreme Court decision put a formal stamp of approval on the separate-but-equal doctrine that justified substandard facilities for blacks. It held sway until it was overruled by the landmark desegregation case *Brown v. Board of Education* in 1954.)

"People tend to forget that we had two big Red scares in this country." (President Woodrow Wilson's attorney general, A. Mitchell Palmer, started the first one back in 1919, and it was a doozy. The execution of anarchists Nicola Sacco and Bartolomeo Vanzetti, which followed their convictions in the early twenties, is usually attributed to the cultivated hysteria of this period.)

"You know how it is—we believe what we want to believe. You'll still hear people say, for instance, that JFK's father bought the 1960 election for him—based on the theory that the Daley forces in

Chicago delivered the state for the Democrats in 1960." (Kennedy needed 269 electoral votes to win; even if Illinois had gone to Nixon, he still would have logged 276.)

When You Want to Change the Subject...

Easy. Just take an informed guess at who was president at *around* the same time as the issue under discussion; then compare that president's problem with a current dilemma facing the present resident of 1600 Pennsylvania Avenue—one you're comfortable talking about—and move into a discussion of current events.

Words to the Wise

You should probably try to choose *one* major topic to which you can always return with relative confidence in any discussion of American history. My vote: the Civil War. (*See separate entry:* "The Civil War.")

HOW TO IMPRESS ANYBODY ABOUT

Baseball

Just as there are dog people and cat people, there are people who like baseball and people who...well, don't like baseball. If you fall into the latter category, but are spending time with someone who falls into the former category, you'll probably want to get up to speed quickly. Here's a painless review of the Grand Old Game.

The Straight Scoop

Baseball is a sport involving balls, bats, and gloves, distantly derived from the old British game of rounders. (Claims that it is a thoroughly and completely American invention don't hold water.) The sport is still rather romantically regarded as America's national pastime, even though its period of primacy in the national psyche ended with the ascent of professional football and basketball (*see separate entries:* "Football" and "Basketball"). Two teams alternate turns at bat and in the field; when in the field, a team of nine defensive players must retire the offense's batters three times, at which point the teams switch roles until at least nine complete cycles (innings) are concluded. It would be nice to report that the rules of baseball as it's played on the professional and amateur levels are simple, but they're not. Rather than try to offer a detailed summary of the rules—which could fill up this book—I'll stand pat with my one-sentence condensation (above) and then move on to some observations on the game's enduring popularity, its lore, and its recent trends.

Baseball, which is popular in such countries as Japan, Cuba, and the Dominican Republic, has a unique hold on the American imagination. It offers an almost perfect balance between individual initiative and group effort. Everyone must contribute as a member of the squad, and victory is usually impossible without teamwork; by the same token, however, each member of the lineup is granted a "moment in the spotlight"—a chance to face off against the opposing team's pitcher, one on one.

Baseball is often dismissed by its detractors as dull, and the pace of the game can certainly be leisurely (especially in its modern form, in which big leaguers seem to take every opportunity to step out of the batter's box and rearrange themselves before the next pitch). But the slowness of the game can reflect an intricacy of plot that's worthy of a great novel or an epic film—and in a pennant race, playoff, or World Series situation, with a whole season on the line, the tension of a tight, well-played baseball game is like nothing else in the world of sports. And with a regular season that runs a hefty 162 games— unlike, for example, pro football's sixteen—the opportunity exists to witness games of staggering meaninglessness…and heart-stopping contests that determine not just the effort on the day in question, but decide the outcome of weeks, months, or years of past contests. (If you're a Boston Red Sox or Chicago Cub fan, your team's every brush with a playoff spot carries with it the emotional baggage of a decades-long struggle to snare a world championship.)

A few of the important events in major league baseball history of which you should be aware:

1903: The first World Series between American League and National League teams is played. The AL Boston Pilgrims defeated the NL Pittsburgh Pirates. Before the advent of the new American League (still referred to as the "junior circuit"), National League champions played world championship series against the top teams in the American Association; when the American Association went belly up, National League teams played for the Temple Cup.

1927: New York Yankee outfielder Babe Ruth slugs 60 home runs, setting a record that will stand until 1961. He is part of a squad that decimates the Pittsburgh Pirates in the World Series and is still regarded as part of perhaps the greatest team in Major League history.

1951: Bobby Thomson's ninth-inning home run against the Dodgers wins the league pennant for the New York Giants, concluding one of the great comebacks in big-league history.

1969: Led by pitcher Tom Seaver, the "Miracle Mets," National League laughingstocks not many years earlier, defeat the Baltimore Orioles in the World Series.

1994: A player's strike stops play in midseason (which is not unprecedented) and eventually costs fans the World Series (which is)

What You Can Say

Baseball fans love to talk about the history of their sport. Here are some insights and opinions you may choose to pass along during conversation.

"The designated hitter rule takes too much strategy out of the game." (This American League innovation, which allows a nonfielding batter to stand in for the pitcher each time he comes to bat, is still taboo in the National League. Pitchers generally make anemic batters. Purists—of which you will be one once you weigh in with this opinion— say the rule adds offense at the expense of strategy and complexity.)

"The great New York Yankee dynasty was really a series of dynasties, with the team reinventing itself in waves as the need arose." (Gaps in the fabled period of New York Yankee pennant dominance occurred from 1929 to 1931 and from 1944 to 1946.)

"One of the most famous numbers in baseball—Babe Ruth's 714 home runs—would have been different if he'd played in the modern era." (Ruth hit a home run in 1918 that, under prevailing rules, was credited only as a triple. At the time, a game-winning hit could not score more than the single run needed for a margin of victory, and that run always ended the game. With the score tied, Ruth hit a home run with a man on first, but was awarded a three-base hit.)

When You Want to Change the Subject...

Start talking about Jackie Robinson's heroic 1947 season, in which Robinson stood tall in the face of catcalls and occasional death threats to take his place as the first black major leaguer of the twentieth century. When he broke in with the Brooklyn Dodgers, Robinson contributed to the inauguration of a new era in American race relations. A discussion of race, social change, or examples of extraordinary personal courage will be fairly easy to navigate from this point.

Words to the Wise

Don't mention the names Bill Buckner or Bob Stanley to Red Sox fans unless you want to inspire torrents of grief. (These two Boston players were involved in the infamous sixth-game 1986 World Series collapse that saw the Red Sox, poised to clinch their first championship since 1918, squander a two-run lead and eventually lose the game to the New York Mets. They lost the Series itself in the next game.)

Basketball

Dr. James Naismith invented it in 1891; formal rules were established in 1892; the Olympics included the game as a sport in 1936; and the world has pretty much been bowing in its direction ever since. Worldwide, the game is exceeded in popularity only by soccer. Basketball's global appeal is probably the result of a relatively simple set of rules, a fast-paced style that can be adapted to just about any playing conditions, and its status as a sport you can play during the winter without too much hassle or preparation.

Here are some insights for those who are still wondering what all the fuss is about.

The Straight Scoop

Object: Put the basketball (a big bouncy thing roughly 30 inches in circumference) through the appropriate metal hoop; one is suspended at each end of a rectangular court. Pick five of your guys to go up against five of their guys. If you want to move the basketball from one point to another, you can either pass it to a teammate or dribble it by bouncing it as you run. Catch it with two hands, and then start dribbling if you want—but once you touch the ball again with both hands, you've got to shoot or pass. Don't step out of bounds with the ball, or the other team gets it. Don't spend more than three seconds in the painted rectangle beneath the opposing team's basket if your team has the ball. Step behind the big, vaguely semicircular line painted outside that rectangle and shoot if you want to score three points, instead of two—and if you're feeling lucky. Don't get caught bumping or elbowing people too much, or your team will pay, either by yielding the other side one-point foul shots or by losing possession of the ball. (Theoretically, basketball is not a contact sport, and anyone who muscles an opposing player will be called for a foul. But theory has its limits.) Get caught for bumping, elbowing, or otherwise manhandling people too much and you'll "foul out" of the game. (For the pros it's six fouls and you're out.)

That's basketball in a nutshell. It takes a minute or two to learn...and a lifetime, as the saying goes, to master.

In the United States, serious basketball (as opposed to the occasionally intense amateur matches conducted in driveways, school gymnasiums, and schoolyards) generally comes in college and pro varieties. These days, both are matters of reverent devotion by legions of fans. In certain areas of the United States (Indiana comes to mind), high school basketball appears to have been accepted by state authorities as a major religion.

For our purposes, we'll focus on the pro game. The National Basketball Association, or NBA, was founded in 1949, and was, for many years, marked by low-scoring games and a playing style that seems, to modern eyes, almost painfully slow. Things heated up considerably in later years, particularly with the advent of the game clock and Wilt Chamberlain—a huge, exceptionally gifted athlete, who revolutionized the offensive game (once scoring 100 points in a single contest), and made the NBA's courts safe for seven-footers. At about the same time, fan interest in the sport started to explode in a manner strangely similar to one of Chamberlain's thundering scoring dunks. The impact of the new approach Chamberlain brought to the game—both for players and the national audience—can hardly be overemphasized; the only recent innovation of comparable status may be the successful 1997 launch of a professional women's league, the WNBA. Wilt is best regarded as a Babe Ruth–like figure who divides the history of his game into fairly neat "before him" and "after him" segments.

Basketball is a team sport, but nowadays its fans tend to focus in on the individual achievements of its superstars, and with good reason. Some of those stars have provided the most exciting visual fireworks in all of sports. In addition to the aforementioned Chamberlain, standout NBA performers have included: Bill Russell (heart of the original Boston Celtics dynasties of the fifties and sixties); Kareem Abdul-Jabbar (the all-time scoring leader, and famous practitioner of the sky hook); Julius Erving (who started his career in the upstart American Basketball Association and turned slam-dunking the ball into high art); Magic Johnson (dazzling playmaker and scoring machine for the great Los Angeles Lakers teams of the eighties and nineties); and Larry Bird (the tough, smart, unrelenting all-hustle leader of the great Boston Celtics teams of the same period). Let's see, now, did I leave anyone out? Oh, yes. On the off chance you've been visiting another solar system for the past decade years or so, I should bring you up to date: there is a gentleman by the name of Michael Jordan whose extraordinary skills are currently on display with the Chicago Bulls. Jordan, who has, as of this writing, led his team to five NBA titles and is favored to do exactly the same thing for as long as he continues playing, is the recipient of vast amounts of media hype and endorsement dollars, owing to the well-publicized fact that he's widely regarded as the greatest player in the history of the game. There's a reason Jordan receives all the attention and adulation he does. He *is* in fact the greatest player in the history of the game.

What You Can Say

"Oh, for the days when the Olympics meant real competition for U.S. basketball teams." (It's quite stylish these days to pine for the days when U.S. Olympic teams, which for many years could not feature professional players, actually faced meaningful competition. If your companion encourages you to elaborate...)

"Who can forget the 1972 finals against the Soviet team?" (Extremely suspect officiating near the end of the game led to a heartbreaking loss for the Americans. Referees kept finding reasons to put new seconds onto the clock for the Russians.)

"My choice for the greatest NBA team of all time? It might have to be that '86 Celtics squad—the one with Bird, Walton, McHale, and Parish. But remember, we're talking about the greatest team—not the team with the most dominant superstar." (The 1986 Boston team was indeed a superbly assembled, well-coordinated machine—a remarkable, thoroughly unselfish ensemble that worked as a single unit with devastating efficiency. The coach, if you're pressed to identify him, was K. C. Jones.)

When You Want to Change the Subject...

Point out that Chamberlain was a breakthrough star like no other in the history of the game. It took pro basketball a few years to catch up to him; there's a story, perhaps apocryphal, that a stunned referee once whistled Chamberlain for a foul after a dunk, simply because the ref had never seen anyone score like that before.

You can then focus the conversation on other figures who radically, and publicly, redefined the limits of the "game" being played at the time. Ask for nominees. (Your own list might include Pablo Picasso, Mahatma Gandhi, Walt Disney, John Lennon, or Albert Einstein.)

Words to the Wise

Don't start singing the praises of Michael Jordan (or, for that matter, Magic Johnson or Kareem Abdul-Jabbar) as the game's greatest player while you're visiting Boston. To those who reside in or near the Hub of the Universe, old Blood and Guts, Larry Bird, will always be the best the game has ever seen. But people are sentimental in that part of the country. Or so I'm told.

HOW TO IMPRESS ANYBODY ABOUT

Cigars

As of this writing, the cigar has made one of the more remarkable pop culture comebacks: In a firmly antismoking era, puffing on a Corona is suddenly hip again.

Because the stogie now appears to be more popular than ever, it's probably a good idea to be able to hold your own in a smoke-filled room—and to be able to separate the cigar-smoking frat boys from the true aficionados. Here's a quick overview of the cigar: how to distinguish what people are smoking, how they go about smoking it, and what you can say while you're waiting for someone to open the window.

The Straight Scoop

For about four hundred years, the cigar meant wealth, power, and status—not to mention a taste for the finer things in life. In the 1960s, big cigars seemed to be synonymous with the Establishment, and that wasn't always a compliment. The fine hand-rolled cigar had become a large brown tube of smelly leaves, as opposed to the smaller hand-rolled smokes of a generation before. Then there was the whole cancer thing. It wasn't long before people started getting distinctly nervous about anything with ashes and tobacco. Cigars weren't cool anymore, even if JFK had enjoyed his.

Everything goes in cycles, though. The Belushis, Schwarzenegger, Willis, Stallone: Suddenly everyone in Hollywood was lighting up, building not just humidors, but humidor rooms—and starting their own smoking clubs. If you find yourself unexpectedly in the middle of one of these, it's good to have some idea of what people will expect from you. Herewith, then, are a few brief words on how to select and smoke a cigar.

The handrolled cigar should be appreciated in much the same way one might enjoy a classic poem, a fine wine, or a painting. It should be approached with reverence. (Most insiders agree that the actual smoking of the cigar is almost secondary.) The key word here is "slow." Make your every action in relation to the cigar one element in a very thoughtful, deliberate process.

The prelighting rituals count for a great deal. Since there is a certain amount of machismo in the cigar world, I would advise you not to choose a cigar that is too small. I'd select a Macanudo, which is mild but not dainty. A woman may look chic holding a panatela or a *très petite* corona. If you're feeling daring you might pick a Lonsdale, which is a size larger. But remember: If the cigar is so huge it just makes you look silly, pick something else.

When in a private home, a humidor (or as the great unwashed sometimes refer to it, "that fancy box for holding cigars") will be held open for you, allowing you to choose from the owner's selection. Take a moment to peruse the choices. Look for a wrapper (the outer leaf that holds the cigar together) that is intact and has a nice sheen.

Nobody wants you fingering the chocolates in the chocolate box too much, and, by the same token, nobody wants you pawing all the cigars in the humidor. Take a long look, pick the one you want, and stick to it. (Real aficionados can tell a goodtasting cigar by sight.) Be patient as you try to light the thing—rolling it in your fingers to get it going on all sides, not just one corner of the stogie.

What You Can Say

"You know, it's been said that a cigar is enjoyed as much with the fingers as it is with the mouth." (Before you light up, hold the cigar up to your ear to listen for a crackle that would signal it's too dry, and then, slowing, pass the cigar under your nose and inhale deeply. This action tells the smoker nothing of consequence about the taste you're about to experience, but it does show that you appreciate cigars in their purest form—unlit.)

"Mmm, lovely leaf. Nice sheen." (Then nod approvingly. When selecting the cigar, make sure the leaf doesn't have too many visible veins; they reduce the pleasure of the contact of the smooth wrapper with your mouth.)

When in a cigar store with someone you want to impress, be sure to say, "What's good today?" (One possible indicator of the quality is the cigar's price. A higher cost doesn't always means a better quality cigar, but it's a pretty good bet.)

"I've found that adding a small sponge in a tiny dish of cognac to the humidor keeps the moisture level right—and improves the flavor of the smoke." (To show your concern for moisture in the cigar, hold it horizontally and squeeze it gently, feeling for a "give" to the cigar. If the cigar appears spongy it probably means that the moisture level in the humidor has been set too high. This will make the cigar harder to light.)

"My favorite cigar guillotine is the Magnum 44." (Yes, they're really called guillotines. There are many tools on the market for cutting the end of the cigar off. Biting is not considered chic because of the tobacco that's left on the biter's teeth, and because of the general Wild West saloon atmosphere the practice involves. The Magnum 44 comes shaped like a bullet but twists open to produce a small elegant circular cutter. With a simple twist, it leaves a neat, perfect opening.)

And here are a few great things you can say about any good cigar you're smoking:

"A nice woodiness on the palate."

"You know, I believe I detect a solid citrus core, it's a refreshing change of pace."

"It has a nice, slightly spicy character, with a hint of cocoa bean."

When You Want to Change the Subject...

Try this: "I think it was Marc Alyn who wrote, 'The cigar smoker, like the perfect lover or the bagpipe player, is a calm man, slow and sure of his wind.' If that's not a ringing endorsement of cigar smoking, I don't know what is. But I think I'd rather be a great lover than a great bagpipe player, wouldn't you?" With any luck, people will now begin talking about sex. You're on your own at that point.

Words to the Wise

Don't allow anyone else to assist you in lighting your cigar. Among those in the know, this is a sign of (unflattering) dependence on the other person. Also: Don't mention anything about the most superb cigars being rolled on the thighs of young Cuban maidens. Those new to the worship of cigars love to pass along this old tale, but the real insiders know it's not true.

HOW TO IMPRESS ANYBODY ABOUT

The Civil War

Historic obsession? This is the biggie—at least as far as America is concerned. (For an overview of the country's development from colonial days onwards, see the separate entry on American History.)

Remember that major PBS documentary series on the Civil War a few years back? Remember how Shelby Foote weighed in with the opinion that an understanding of the Civil War is essential to any fundamental understanding of the American experience as a whole? Well, he was right. So, now that I've raised the bar to an impossible height, it's time to give you all the inside information you need about the pivotal American event. In a couple of pages. All right, maybe it's not *all* the information you need, but it's enough to pique your curiosity and get you through a cocktail party, *Jeopardy* broadcast, or a lunch with a new acquaintance. I, for one, am content to busy myself with the attainment of such worthy goals.

The Straight Scoop

The long debated, much discussed question of slavery tends to loom large in modern discussions of the Civil War (also known as the War Between the States), as well it should. The contentious matter of whether one American should be permitted to own another definitely served to heighten long-simmering tensions between Northern and Southern states in the years before the war. It's important to remember, though, that the rights of enslaved blacks were not primary concerns of Northern or Southern politicians as the conflict began. The Southern, or Confederate, states sought to preserve particular states rights—notably the right of states to set definitive policy—regarding both the institution of slavery *and* their own status as members of the Union. (In other words, leaders in the South believed they had the right to secede from the United States.) Northern, or Union, states fought for the principle of a single, indivisible nation, and in opposition to the notion that secession was a legitimate option for any state. Emancipation of the slaves was a subordinate concern at best for the North as the war began, although it emerged as an increasingly important issue as the conflict progressed.

By the time the Union prevailed in 1865, the Southern states had been decimated, and over 600,000 Americans on both sides had lost their lives. Generals Ulysses S. Grant (for the Union) and Robert E. Lee (for the Confederacy) emerged as titanic figures in the struggle.

Here's a condensed chronology:

1860: Republican Abraham Lincoln, facing a divided Democratic party, is elected president with a minority of the popular vote. South Carolina promptly secedes from the Union, charting a path that will eventually be followed by six more Southern states by the time of Lincoln's inauguration, and a total of eleven by the end of the following year. Despite the sudden rash of secessions, Lincoln's fateful election in 1860 does not represent an ascent to power by those seeking to abolish slavery; Lincoln simply regards slavery as morally wrong, is willing to say so, and is opposed to its further extension.

1861: Southern states form the Confederate States of America. Lincoln takes office. The Confederates capture the federal fort at Fort Sumter, South Carolina. The Confederates score another victory at the First Battle of Bull Run.

1862: The remarkably bloody, but indecisive, battle of Shiloh leads to appalling losses on both sides; the battle does, however, pave the way for future Union victories in the west. In the meantime, the Confederates triumph in the Second Battle of Bull Run, and are then checked at Antietam by Union forces. General George McClellan fails to attack the retreating confederates; Lincoln, who had demoted McClellan once before, loses faith in him for good.

1863: Lincoln formally issues the Emancipation Proclamation, freeing slaves under Confederate authority. The proclamation, which has no effect in slave states that opted not to secede, or on slaves held in territory reclaimed by Union forces in recent battles, nevertheless adds an important moral dimension to the war. Just as important, it ensures neutrality from England and France. The Union triumphs at the battle of Gettysburg, bringing Lee's invasion of the North to an end and serving as the turning point of the conflict. After a long siege, Grant captures Vicksburg.

1864: At the battle of Cold Harbor, Lee stalls Grant's advance toward the Confederate capital, Richmond. Union general William Tecumseh Sherman marches through and devastates Georgia, capturing Atlanta.

1865: Lee surrenders to Grant at Appomattox. Lincoln is assassinated in Washington.

After the war, with a strong central government irrevocably established, slavery outlawed, and the question of secession finally resolved in bloody but definitive fashion, deep divisions between Northern and Southern states remained. This grisly war—and the period of Northern occupation that followed it, known as Reconstruction—was a bitterly divisive affair that left profound and long-lasting rifts in the country.

What You Can Say

"I suppose the one indisputable thing one can say about the Civil War is that it was the bloodiest in the country's history—but you have to bear in mind that more soldiers died of disease than from wounds incurred on the battlefield." (Regardless of how they died, however, it's true that more Americans died as a result of the Civil War than any other conflict—and that includes both World Wars.)

"Has there ever been an election like that which took place in 1864?"

(Lincoln found himself running for reelection, during wartime, against the very Union general who had given him endless headaches on the battlefield, George McClellan.)

"However Lincoln's intentions may have been interpreted after the war, the truth is that, for most of his time in office, he was unlikely to be confused with an abolitionist. His primary aim was to restore the Union, not to eliminate slavery." (As noted above, Lincoln's decision to issue the Emancipation Proclamation was more of a shrewd political and diplomatic maneuver than a principled stand against slavery. Slaves in the loyal border states of Delaware, Kentucky, Maryland, and Missouri were unaffected by the decree.)

When You Want to Change the Subject...

Ask your conversational partner to identify an American historical event that rivals the Civil War in importance. (Ther aren't many, but coming up with rival candidates is a fun diversion.)

Words to the Wise

Fundamentally differing interpretations of the war, nearly a century and a half after its conclusion, are still common in discussions between modern-day Northerners and Southerners. Simple rule: Don't press a point simply for the sake of pressing it. You may start some fireworks you didn't mean to start.

The Cold War

A "cold" war is a conflict that, by definition, doesn't result in open military hostility, but is submerged in constant hostility and mutual suspicion. The Cold War, capital C, capital W, was the long-running period of tension between the United States and the Soviet Union (or, as the West so often had it in the fifties, a supposedly monolithic Communist bloc) as they faced off after World War II. Sure, you know how it ended—but how much do you know about what happened before the Soviet empire collapsed and the Berlin Wall came a-tumbling down?

The Straight Scoop

1945: The United States, having defeated the Japanese after dropping atom bombs on the cities of Hiroshima and Nagasaki, entered the postwar period in the unfamiliar position of global superpower. Its ally during the war, the Soviet Union, proved to be tough and recalcitrant during negotiating sessions about the future of postwar Europe in general, and Germany in particular. A period of mutual tension and mistrust (which seemed to build on wariness between Moscow and Washington during the war itself) followed.

The Cold War began in earnest when the Truman administration committed itself to aid non-Communist forces in Greece (1947) during the civil war there. Soviet influence over governments in Eastern Europe was a cause of grave concern to Western nations, but these were by no means the only hot spots—concern over Communist advances in other parts of the world also troubled Western leaders, who embraced a policy of "containment." American strategists and spokesmen often saw the Communist movement as more global, monolithic, and singleminded than it actually was. Even so, the Soviet domination of European nations led to the establishment of massive Western military, economic, and diplomatic initiatives, but not to outright war. The Americans organized NATO, the North Atlantic Treaty Organization; the Soviets established the Warsaw Pact. Once the Soviets developed their own atomic weapons (1949), a race between the superpowers to develop arsenals of mass destruction picked up speed.

The Cold War was played out against the constant possibility that it might (gulp) heat up. Given the destructive powers of the countries involved, that was enough to get anybody a little nervous. Tense moments of the Cold War included:

- The Berlin Airlift (1948–1949), during which Western planes dropped supplies to the blockaded citizens of West Berlin, which remained one half of a divided city. (Berlin was a potential flashpoint until the years 1970 to 1973, when a series of agreements acknowledged the borders and authorities of the competing parties.)

- The decision of Soviet leaders to invade Hungary (1956) and Czechoslovakia (1968) to choke off reform efforts in both countries.

- The Soviet union's 1960 downing of an American military reconnaissance plane (supposedly on a "weather observation mission") that had violated Russian airspace to take photos of military sites. Gary Powers, the pilot, was captured and held prisoner for two years; he was eventually exchanged for a Soviet agent held by the United States. The Powers affair resulted in the cancellation of a 1960 summit meeting in Paris between Soviet leader Krushchev and president Eisenhower. Krushchev denounced the American spy flights, returned to a combative stance with the West after having sent relatively conciliatory signals, and launched a Soviet arms buildup that lasted into the 1970s.

- The Cuban Missile Crisis (1962), when nuclear catastrophe loomed until the Soviet leadership agreed to dismantle secretly constructed missile installations in Cuba.

There were more prolonged struggles, as well. American efforts to forestall the rise of Communist governments in Asia led to a bloody stalemate in the Korean War in the 1950s and a prolonged, ill-conceived, and ultimately futile military struggle in Vietnam in the 1960s and early 1970s. The doctrine of containment proved a difficult and very costly idea to put into practice.

In 1972, President Nixon—who had launched his political career as one of the most virulent domestic anti-Communists—made diplomatic overtures to China, thereby making a formal acknowledgment that the so-called Sino-Soviet bloc had deep divisions. A detente period of lessening tension and respect for established spheres of influence arose between U.S. and Soviet governments during the seventies, but did not endure.

A tricky question arose during the Cold War: How many times could you possibly want to destroy civilization? Ludicrous excesses in destructive capacity led to fitful efforts at arms limitation, but never to any meaningful attempt at disarmament during the Cold War. In 1979, the Soviet invasion of Afghanistan in support of a Marxist government deepened existing rifts between the United States and the Soviet Union. The election of Ronald Reagan in 1980 sharply reemphasized the anti-Soviet aspect of American foreign policy; Reagan's rhetoric against the "evil [Soviet] empire" evoked the early tensions and the polarization of the Truman era, but is now credited by many as a necessary prelude to the eventual Soviet collapse. At the time, however, it left some people (including me) feeling just a little out of sorts, reviving, as it appeared to do, the possibility of the whole nuclear apocalypse thing.

Mikhail Gorbachev's selection in 1985 as general secretary of the Communist Party of the Soviet Union signaled the rise of *perestroika* (restructuring) and a seemingly new phase of Soviet rule; Gorbachev's attempts to revitalize the sluggish Soviet economy, however, were unsuccessful. Internal pressures mounted within an increasingly troubled Soviet Union, and the system of satellite Soviet nations began to fall apart. The Berlin Wall, and with it the pro-Soviet East German regime, collapsed in 1989. The Soviets declined to exercise a veto over American-led military efforts against Iraq in 1991. A ham-handed coup attempt against Gorbachev collapsed in the face of popular opposition late in the same year, and the period of Soviet Communist dominance officially ended shortly thereafter.

The international picture that emerged after the tumultuous final phase of Communist dominance in the Soviet Union took a little getting used to for Westerners who had accepted the Cold War as a grim and inevitable fact of geopolitical life. The Communist Party of the Soviet Union was outlawed. Nations of Eastern Europe that had once been forced to submit to Communist dictates emerged as independent countries. And (perhaps most remarkable of all) nations like Bieloruss and Ukraine, for nearly seventy years part of the Soviet empire (and the empire of the czars before that), emerged as independent, sovereign countries. If the Cold War was to be defined as the period of global struggle for dominance between the United States and the Soviet Union, it had apparently concluded in victory for the West. (*See separate entry:* "American History.")

What You Can Say

"Whatever people may feel now about the Rosenbergs, they can't deny that the controversy around the case illustrated the depth of the anti-Soviet public feeling in the early Fifties." (Julius and Ethel Rosenberg were executed in 1953 for conspiring to pass military secrets to the Soviets; to this day, opinions vary widely as to the treatment they received for their actions. Although contemporary passions were aroused on both sides of the case, public outrage at the Rosenbergs was intense and prolonged.)

"Of course, the turning point in the Cuban Missile Crisis came when Kennedy chose to ignore Khruschev's hard-line cable, and respond instead to the message it had been meant to supersede." (Kennedy, aware that Khruschev had been pressured by elements within the

Kremlin, chose to respond to the more conciliatory of the two messages he received.)

"The Cold War was as dark, full of reversals, and complicated as the most prominent American politician it produced." (Warning: Don't launch this one unless you're prepared to engage in a discussion of the extraordinary career of that early Red-baiter, late master diplomat, inspired strategist, perpetual self-destroyer, and perpetual self-inventor, Richard Nixon.)

A brief side note: Anybody who claims to know everything about the Cold War, in its domestic and international dimensions, is bluffing. It's like *Hamlet* or the Bible—you can study it for a lifetime and not catch all the dimensions. Shift the discussion to what you know, and rest assured that you've got every right to hold your own opinion.

When You Want to Change the Subject...

Pick a period in time that carries vivid memories for you, and then mention the degree to which the Cold War did (or didn't) exert a powerful influence on you. Children who went to grammar school during the fifties and early sixties may have vivid memories of air-raid drills and the like; those who went to school in later years probably won't. A discussion of how the Cold War affected individual families in different periods may be your best bet to move the conversation to other topics.

Words to the Wise

Some Cold War topics—the treatment of the Rosenbergs, the guilt or innocence of State Department official Alger Hiss, who was accused of acting as an agent for the Soviets in the 1930s—still stir up intense partisan debate. (Both the Rosenbergs and Hiss were convicted, Hiss for perjury.) Don't make blithe pronouncements or sweeping statements about such matters unless you're prepared to back them up at length. Personally, I'd let someone else duke it out for a while and just listen.

HOW TO IMPRESS ANYBODY ABOUT

Einstein's Theory of Relativity

The beauty of taking on a conversation about Einstein's Theory of Relativity is that, in most cases, virtually no one will be in a position to contradict what you say. Let's face it. Everyone will be uncertain; it's just a question of who's prepared the best material. So use what you want from what follows, then say it loudly and confidently, look 'em right in the eye, and smile. Then, if you feel like scoring some extra points, you can express wonder that it took the folks on the Nobel committee sixteen years to award Einstein the prize for physics. (He won it in 1921.)

The Straight Scoop

Not surprisingly, Albert Einstein was constantly asked to summarize his Theory of Relativity in a brief way, "that the layperson would understand." Einstein would answer with words to the following effect, which I suggest you appropriate.

"If you promise not to take the answer all that seriously," Einstein would say, "and if you promise to think of what I'm about to say as a kind of joke based on the Theory of Relativity, then yes, I can give a brief description of it. Scientists once believed that, if all material things disappeared from the universe, time and space would remain. But according to the Theory of Relativity, time and space disappear along with the material things."

Let's say that explanation isn't enough for you. Let's say you want

32

to be able to talk in a little more detail about the specifics of the Theory of Relativity. (Who knows why you would want to do such a thing, but let's say you do.)

The best way to approach this is to begin with the rules of force and motion developed by Sir Isaac Newton. (*See entry:* "Newtonian Physics.") For all of the eighteenth and a good chunk of the nineteenth century, these laws did a great job of explaining how all the observed physical entities of the universe acted in relation to one another. Along about the middle of the nineteenth century, however, scientists started having problems. They kept finding things that didn't square with Newton's laws. The thing that kept giving them the biggest headache was light. They couldn't understand exactly how it moved through space. People batted ideas around for a while, but nothing anyone suggested really explained away all the questions the scientists had.

Einstein solved the problem by redefining space. Using the Theory of Relativity, space and time were no longer seen as separate entities, but as components of a four-dimensional, space-time continuum. His Theory of Special Relativity (1905) held that nature's laws are the same in different moving systems, and that the speed of light is a constant, regardless of the speed of the person observing it or the direction from which the light comes.

What You Can Say

Bewildered? Just say this:

"The Theory of Special Relativity answered the questions the scientists had been confronting about how light worked—and it revolutionized physics, because it did everything Newton's laws did, and then some." Einstein's (really) new and improved set of rules took physics to another level. The Theory of Special Relativity could predict the outcome of everyday physical actions in roughly the same way Newton's laws could, and it also gave more accurate answers when applied to situations Newton hadn't contemplated. (Such as what happens when a moving body approaches the speed of light. Short answer: What we normally think of as space and time get all wacky.)

The Theory of General Relativity (circa 1916) dealt mostly with gravitation. In certain situations (mostly of interest to scientists) in which Newtonian laws had failed, this theory accurately explained, among other things, the ways certain bodies in the solar system acted.

When You Want to Change the Subject...

Make a joke about how you've developed your own theory of relativity, as a direct result of relatives who take up more than the customary allotment of time and space. Then start making fun of your overweight Uncle Harold.

Words To The Wise

If you notice the objects around you becoming surrealistically misshapen, you are talking about the Theory of Relativity too fast. For your own well-being, stop before you reach the speed of light.

English Grammar and Usage

The best advice anyone can pass along to a writer eager to learn the basics of English grammar is to buy a copy of *The Elements of Style,* by William Strunk Jr. and E. B. White. The following summary assumes that you've lost or been separated from your own copy of Strunk and White, and are looking for a brisk overview of the best ways to avoid the most common writing errors.

The Straight Scoop

Subjects have to agree with verbs. Even when words come between a subject and its verb, the number of the verb *must* match that of its subject. The following sentence, for instance, is grammatically correct: "The many-layered joy of being young in Brooklyn—the schoolyard games, the sounds, the visits to Ebbets Field—is etched upon my memory." Replacing the world "is" with the word "are" would be incorrect. A similar problem arises with the common construction "one of." This sentence is correct: "Wendy is one of those writers who are capable of writing grammatically perfect chapters." Replacing the word "are" with the word "is" would be incorrect. The subjects "everybody" and "everyone" take singular verbs: "Everyone in my class is angry because none of us is going to the picnic." (But note that "none" may demand a plural verb when it carries a clear plural sense: "None are so blind as those who will not

35

see." As a general rule, though, "none" means "not one" or "no one" and should be treated as a singular.)

Don't get your subjects mixed up. "Walking into the room, the door struck my knee." Unless the door was doing the walking, the sentence needs to be revised. Make sure clauses match up with the appropriate subject.

Avoid splitting infinitives. Is it always wrong to break up an infinitive verb form by writing, for instance, "to boldly go"? Maybe not, but unless you've got a really great reason for emphasizing the adverb in question, you're better off writing "to go boldly." (Apologies to captains Kirk and Picard.)

Avoid ending sentences with prepositions. "This is the standard all good writers must eventually be measured by." "This is the standard by which all good writers must eventually be measured." I don't know about you, but for this reader, the second version wins hands down. Again, this rule may not apply in every conceivable situation—Winston Churchill is said to have dismissed it as, "The kind of pedantry up with which I will not put"—but it's still a reliable guide to good composition. If ending your sentences with prepositions calls attention to itself—and it usually does—why break this rule needlessly? In most cases, there will be many more graceful strategies you can use to make your point.

Use adverbs properly. An adverb is a word that modifies a verb. So you can say, "Stan looked at me hopefully," because the word "hopefully" modifies the verb "looked." But you should stay away from "Hopefully, Stan will show up this morning." After all, you're not saying that Stan will show up in a hopeful state of mind, but that you hope Stan will show up in the first place! A better way to say this would be "I hope Stan will show up this morning."

Know when to use "that" and when to use "which." I could go into a discussion of restrictive and nonrestrictive pronouns, but to be perfectly honest, I usually have to look up which label applies to which word. I can, however, pass along an easy-to-remember rule that makes intuitive sense, doesn't slow down your work, and virtually always makes your sentence correct: Use "which" immediately after a comma and "that" in other situations. This means you could write "My car, which is blue, is ready to be delivered." That is for when there's only one car and the fact that it's blue is simply added information. Alternatively, you could write, "The car that is blue is ready to be delivered." That's for when there's a number of cars under discussion, and the blueness of the one you're talking about is what sets it apart from the others. You *should not* write "The car which is blue is ready to be delivered"—although many of people do write sentences like that and don't seem to mind the lack of a comma. But you're reading this book because you want to impress others with your knowledge, right?

What You Can Say

Some people tend to think of those who hold forth at length about issues grammatical as insufferable pedants; others simply love discussing matters of English usage and style and will be more than happy to take advantage of the opportunity to do so with you. Regardless of which group you end up with, you'll probably want to have a working knowledge of the following commonly misused word pairs. If you're among word-fiends, knowledge of the following distinctions will serve as something of a membershp card. In other situations, making a big deal about this may or may not make you more popular. It all depends on your attitude. If you don't have to correct someone else's grammar (that is, if you're not working as an editor or in a related capacity), you probably shouldn't be too picky.

"Someone who is *averse* to a certain idea is opposed to it; he or she may be against it because of the possibility it will lead to *adverse* consequences."

"I'm *anxious* about that which worries or unsettles me; I'm *eager* about that which excites or motivates me."

"When a writer *implies* something, she's dropping hints or suggesting; when I *infer* something from what she's written, I'm drawing conclusions—assuming information that she hasn't set out directly."

"The whole *comprises,* or embraces, the parts, that means that we can't say that something 'is comprised of' something else. Usually, what we mean is 'is *composed* of.'"

"When I *flaunt* something, I display it in a gaudy way; when I *flout* a rule, I ignore it with contempt."

"That which *amuses* is humorous, enjoyable, or entertaining; that which *bemuses* bewilders or confuses."

"*Farther* is for distances of physical space; *further* is for discussions of time or degree."

"To say 'A *denotes* B' is to say that A literally means B; but to say 'A *connotes* B' is to say that A suggests, evokes, or signifies B, in addition to A's explicit meaning."

When You Want to Change the Subject...

...do so with caution and humility! Falsely claiming to have (or, worse yet, to be) the final authority on a matter of grammar or usage can make for some ugly transitions. People who know their English love to talk about the subject. They will assume that you love to talk about it just as much as they do and will want to determine precisely why you feel the way you do about a certain subject. Rather than leaving the door open for endless queries by saying something like, "It seems to me that William Safire agreed with me on this, but I can't quite recall when the column ran," you should probably point out that the language we speak is an evolving one, and that accepted standards sometimes change while people aren't looking. After that, you can start making fun of the French, who set up commissions with the apparent aim of keeping their native tongue free from unwanted influences.

Words to the Wise

The standards are different (that is, considerably stricter) for written English than they are for the spoken variety. Trying to correct your conversational companion's perceived grammatical errors on the fly may lead to some awkward moments. Keep the discussion in the abstract—and don't try to assume the role of self-appointed grammar cop during the conversation

HOW TO IMPRESS ANYBODY ABOUT

Exotic (and Not-So-Exotic) Drinks

Nothing impresses the urbane, self-absorbed, continental type like the perfect dry martini, right? Well, imagine how impressed that person will be when you mix one all on your own. If you're trying to hang out with those who have a taste for the "right" drinks, knowing what to drink and when to drink it can gain you points.

So—how can you come across as the one "in the know" when it's time to order or mix drinks? Below, you'll find a few pointers.

The Straight Scoop

First, a little background: An "alcoholic beverage" is any drink that contains ethyl alcohol. (Sounds about as sophisticated as spending your happy hour guzzling from a service-station nozzle, doesn't it?) Of the several types of ethyl alcohol, spirits distilled from grain, grape, fruit, and sugarcane are the most common. There are two main groups of alcoholic beverages, fermented drinks and distilled drinks. The fermented drinks are beers and wines. Spirits, or liquors, are distilled drinks which contain 40-to 50-percent ethyl alcohol. They include brandy, gin, rum, vodka, and whiskey.

The percentage of alcohol in distilled drinks is called the proof. In the United States, the proof is equal to twice the amount of alcohol in the beverage. So a drink that is 100 proof contains 50 percent alcohol.

Here's the skinny on some of the most popular distilled drinks.

Whiskey is a blend of as many as forty kinds of spirits made from different grains. (Scotch is a type of whiskey that comes from Scotland.) Whiskey can be served straight, on the rocks (that is, with ice), or mixed with water. Vodka has very little taste or odor and is usually mixed with orange juice, tomato juice, or tonic water. Liqueurs are made by flavoring brandy, gin, or other spirits with fruits and flowers, and can be served straight or on the rocks. Gin is a flavored mixture of alcohol and is usually mixed with juice. Rum is made from the syrup of sugarcane and mixed with juices or cola. Lastly, brandy is distilled from grape wine, and can be served straight or mixed with another spirit.

What You Can Say

"I know a great drink for after dinner: the Dark Secret." (Fill a glass with ice, an ounce and a half of cognac or brandy, half an ounce of Amaretto, and stir.)

"Would you like your martini dry or very dry?" (For the standard version: Fill a glass with ice, two ounces of gin, and half an ounce of dry vermouth. For a "dry martini" use less vermouth. For a "very dry martini" use hardly any at all. Stir gently and garnish with lemon twists or one or two green olives—or, to create a Gibson, use cocktail onions.)

"You look like you've had The Day—I'll mix you an After Five." (That's half an ounce of coffee liqueur, half an ounce of Irish cream, and half an ounce of peppermint schnapps.)

"Care for a drink that doesn't apologize for being a drink?" (Try the Colorado Bulldog. All you do is fill a glass with ice, add one ounce of vodka, one ounce of coffee liqueur, and two ounces of cola. Stir and serve.)

"The Bad Attitude is a drink not to be messed with." (Fill a glass with ice, then add one ounce of coconut rum, one ounce of spiced rum, and two ounces of pineapple juice. Shake. Strain the drink and put it in a chilled glass.)

"Care for a Pond Scum? It isn't as disgusting as it sounds." (Prove it.

Fill a glass with ice, two ounces of vodka, and a splash of soda water. Then float a quarter ounce of Irish cream on the top.)

"Here's the toughest glass of ice tea you'll ever encounter. It's called an Ice Pick." (Pretty straightforward, too. Fill a glass with ice, two ounces of vodka, and ice tea. Flavor with sugar and or lemon as desired. Garnish with a lemon.)

"The most important drink recipe I've ever come across? Easy: Hangover Be Gone." (That's one B-complex vitamin downed with a glass of soda water with five to ten drops of bitters in it.)

When You Want to Change the Subject...

If everyone at the bar or attending your party has had enough to drink, changing the subject should really be no problem. No one will remember what they were talking about anyway. Pick a topic, any topic, and run with it.

Words to the Wise

Never ask the bartender for anything that hops, skips, is naked, kisses, is slippery, is (literally or figuratively) frozen, comes with an umbrella, is served in a tiki glass, is on fire or begins with the letters x, y, or z. When in doubt, try ordering scotch and soda. (Not, as a friend of mine once requested on his very first visit to a bar, scotch and orange juice. Yuck.)

Finally, drink responsibly. If you're in no condition to drive, give the keys to someone who is

Film Noir

These movies are what lots of people mean when they say that Hollywood "doesn't make 'em like that anymore." That's just a bit too sentimental for me. The dark, brooding film noir masterpieces of years past eventually spawned a number of modern movies in basically the same genre, many of them just about as good as the originals. So here's your five-minute rundown on the genre that just won't quit: dark movies, or, as the French prefer to put it, film noir.

The Straight Scoop

There are two main groups of movies that fans may be talking about when they talk about film noir: "classic film noir" and the more recent "film noir in color" category. That second classification seems to be a contradiction in terms, but what's at issue is not necesarily the presence or absence of color on the screen, but the underlying emotion, dialogue, pacing, and visual style of the piece. Anyway, here's the rundown on both groups, sweetheart.

Classic film noir refers to the original wave of tough, glamorous, coolly cynical pictures from Hollywood's golden era, typically crime dramas shot in black and white (mostly black). These pictures had a somber, fatalistic feel that evoked a world on the prowl. The world of film noir is a world where heroes are not necessarily virtuous, seductive dames are rarely looking out for the best interests of those heroes, institutions of authority are not to be trusted, and endings are not necessarily happy. Frequently, the game is fixed. The directors of these hypnotically grim, deliciously alluring pictures had a genius for making the most of the limitations of the time. They took low budgets and minimal sets...and somehow used the absence of hard cash to fashion a new, dark-toned cinematic visual language, one that was perfectly in keeping with the insecurity, paranoia, and ambivalence of modern life. They took a prudish production code and used it as an excuse to raise ambiguity, implication, and double meaning to a high art. They took potboiler plots and managed to make them support surrealistic flashbacks and dream sequences. And, every now and then, they took notably cheesy dialogue and somehow got their actors to make it work.

Most film buffs agree that the classic film noir period begins with John Huston's *The Maltese Falcon* (1941) and closes with Orson Welles's *Touch of Evil* (1958), although there were several important precursor noir films that seem to merit some kind of recognition, such as *I Am a Fugitive from a Chain Gang* (1932). Whenever it started, the noir movement gave rise to some of the moodiest, grittiest, most gloriously twisted work the Hollywood studio system ever produced. I don't have room to list even a tenth of the great films of the period here, but here's a roll call of a few of the most memorable you can use as an impressive conversational ploy: *High Sierra* (1941), *Casablanca* (1942), *Double Indemnity* (1944), *Laura* (1944), *Notorious* (1944), *Spellbound* (1945), *The Postman Always Rings Twice* (1946), *Dark Passage* (1947), *Lady from Shanghai* (1948), *The Lost Weekend* (1945), *White Heat* (1949), *Sunset Boulevard* (1950), *The Asphalt Jungle* (1950), *Strangers on a Train* (1951), *D.O.A.* (1952), and *The Big Sleep* (1953). Let it be noted, too, that Orson Welles's 1942 masterwork *Citizen Kane* had a major role in inspiring the distinctive look and feel of the film noir classics of the 1940s. (Side note: Missed one or more of these pictures? Take a powder—make your way over to the local video outlet and rent yourself a classic. You'll be glad you did. And now, back to our feature.)

Color film noir is an umbrella term that describes color films that evoke the same dark, morally ambiguous world of the originals. The term usually refers to movies made some years after the initial wave of film noir pictures—although it's worth noting that some color films of the fifties, like Hitchcock's *Vertigo* (1958), were strongly influenced by the original black-and-white film noir tradition. Successful color film noir entries of later vintage include *Chinatown* (1974), *Farewell, My Lovely* (1975), *Body Heat* (1981), *Blade Runner* (1982), *Pulp Fiction* (1995), and *L.A. Confidential* (1997). No, it's not your imagination. There haven't been as many really good color film noir pictures as Hollywood gave us in the black-and-white days. But we can always hope for a comeback. Who knows. We may get one yet, sweetheart.

What You Can Say

This one's easy. Just quote some of the can't-miss lines from the pictures themselves. Here's a representative sampling. (Once you work your way over to the video store, you can develop your own list of personal favorites):

"I want what she's got. All of it. I want her house, her name, her man. And I want them now. Tonight." Hazel Brooks in *Sleep, My Love* (1948).

"You're getting a big kick out of making me feel cheap, aren't you? Well, maybe I had it coming." Dorothy Patrick in *Follow Me Quietly* (1949).

"So I'm no good. But I'm no worse than anybody else." Van Heflin in *The Prowler* (1951).

"I can be framed easier than Whistler's mother." Mark Stevens in *The Dark Corner* (1946).

"It took more than one man to change my name to Shanghai Lily." Marlene Dietrich in *Shanghai Express* (1932).

"She was a charming middle-aged lady with a face like a bucket of mud. I gave her a drink. She was a gal who'd take a drink if she had to knock you down to get the bottle." Dick Powell in *Murder, My Sweet* (1944)

"You know how to whistle, don't you, Steve? You just put your lips together and blow." Lauren Bacall in *To Have and Have Not* (1945).

When You Want to Change the Subject...

Mention that leading women in classic film noir are almost always strong, goal-oriented, sexually confident people, and that—surprise, surprise—they're usually punished by the Powers That Be as a direct result. You can then move into a discussion of feminism, media stereotypes, changing sexual mores, or classic James Bond movies, which had a nasty habit of contriving punishments for women who were weak, aimless, sexually manipulated people. Talk about your no-win situation. Maybe you could just talk about Ellen DeGeneres for a while and let everyone relax.

Words to the Wise

Like lots of formal terminology, the precise limits of the term "film noir" are subject to debate and interpretation. (There is, for instance, a good deal of inconclusive debate on the subject of what, precisely, the first film noir feature was.) Don't get too hung up on the labels—and don't be surprised if someone holds a different opinion than you do about the films under discussion.

HOW TO IMPRESS ANYBODY ABOUT

Fine Wines

Look up the word pompous in a really big dictinary, and the odds are good that you'll find a reference that reads "see wine snob."

There may be times when you want to impress some wine expert or other, or pass as one yourself. When in Rome (a fine place to buy wine, by the way) you must sometimes, as the phrase has it, do as the Romans do. Let's face it, watching those *Frasier* reruns may not do the trick. The observations below may be just what you need.

The Straight Scoop

The three most common terms you're likely to encounter when assessing wines are red (these wines use the entire crushed grape during fermentation), white (only the juice is reserved), and rosé (skins are extracted from the process after fermentation has begun, leaving the wine with a pink tone). Another important pair of distinctions: Dry and sweet. The drier a wine is, the more of the grape sugar has been permitted to ferment into alcohol.

The easy way to sound as though you know what you are talking about is to appropriate some of the in-crowd text yourself. There are a wealth of terms you can use as snobby shortcuts to show off what you know (or, to be more accurate, just got done reading about in this book). These words will get you at least halfway there. But remember, many have tried to spout a few adjectives and only come away sounding like poseurs. Don't be one of them. Deliver your remarks appropriately—that is to say, remember to, well, belittle the wine, no matter how much you like it. To the expert, there is no such things as a perfect glass of wine. So when you're assessing wines, don't forget that there are poor wines, nice wines, good wines, even exceptional wines, but never perfect wines.

A bad wine is poor or, even more authoritative-sounding, "an unfortunate wine." I love that phrase. It makes it sound as if the stuff in your glass were a child of poor breeding. An old wine that has not aged well has become "senile" or—(even worse)—has "died"! There is one exception to this never-praise-anything-that-comes-in-a-bottle-too-highly rule: You may refer to a wine that you drank a very, very long time ago, as perfect. It may make sense to you to discuss one wine that you remember longingly and with a certain melancholy, like your first lover. Do so with the hint of a tear in one eye.

The ancient Greeks made wine by fermenting the grapes in clay jars coated with pine tar. The Greeks also added handfuls of pungent herbs to the mix. The result (which you can still buy) can be quite a shock to the untrained palette. But hey, if it was good enough for Plato, it's good enough for us.

Near-global participation in the art of making wine has done much to further its popularity since the days of Greek vintners. Pretty much everyone makes wine today—Egypt, Peru, China, even Texas—and, for the most part, there are products with some basic appeal from just about every part of the world. The exception to remember: the English, who have done for wine about what they've done for blood pudding. I should note, however, that the Brits have historically been knowledgeable enthusiasts for wine produced in other countries. This fondness for the fruit of the vine apparently goes back to Henry V. Speaking of the English, members of the Monty Python comedy troupe did much to pooh-pooh Australian table wines, but in truth there are many "nice" ones out there from Down Under.

The Germans make many wonderful wines. If the taste isn't enough to impress you, the zealous use of vowels and consonants should. A bottle of Trockenbeerenauslese can sell for more than $125. Believe me, it's money well spent—that is if you can wrap your tongue around the name to order it correctly.

The French are generally considered the world's premier wine-makers, but don't let the fancy names and the high prices intimidate you. When in doubt, order the most expensive variety you can afford and make it a rosé; that goes with everything. If it's champagne you're looking for, remember cheap will give you a headache and expensive will empty your pocket. A bottle of Dom Perignon or Cristal will really set you back, and a bottle of Ohio's cheapest will leave you wishing for a removable head and a dark room to put it in. Go for the middle ground.

This brings up an important question: How do you order wine when you haven't got a clue what to order? The easiest thing to do is order by the price—that is, if it's listed. If no price appears on the menu, you're probably in trouble. This is going to be expensive. Sure you wouldn't rather have a club soda with a twist?

There are two strategies to consider here. One: Throw caution to the wind and pick one about three quarters the way down the page, with a name you're pretty sure you can pronounce correctly. Two: Ask the waiter or wine steward for a recommendation. Then say to your dining companions, "I always ask—sometimes they have a surprising favorite, something for when you're feeling adventurous."

You'll probably be asked to sniff the cork and sample a little bit of the wine. Unless you suspect grave problems, nod intently and with a furrowed brow after each experience.

Bear in mind that there are four main types of wines.

- Natural (or "still") wines—those whose alcohol results entirely from fermentation—are what most of us think of when we think of wine. The big-name wine regions of major winemaking countries tend to predominate here: Burgundy, Bordeaux (France); Moselle (Germany; be sure to pronounce it Moe-zell, rather sternly and with authority); and Chianti (key-aunt-tee) and Veronese (Italy).

- Sparkling wines are the second category. Champagne, remember, can come only from that region in France. Otherwise the wine still sparkles, but it is called sparkling table wine (natch). Examples of non-Champagne sparkling wines include Asti Spumante and

Sekt. Riunite is also a sparkling wine, but be forewarned that a screw-off cap and a free pen offer on the back of the bottle should be considered warning signs.

• Fortified wines are the harder stuff with an alcohol content of 14 to 25 percent. This group would include sherry, port (great with cigars), madeira, and marsala.

• Feeling fancy? Aromatized wines include vermouths and aperitifs. Quinined wines are made with the sweeter vermouths and are great for keeping the old malaria at bay. Examples of aromatized wines include Dubonnet, both the red and the white varieties; Lillet (serve it chilled, with a twist of orange), both the red and the white varieties; and St. Raphael, of which only the red stuff is sold in the United States. (Note: You may want to mention this fact and pine longingly for St. Raphael's white variety if the opportunity presents itself.)

Going to a wine tasting? My advice is to not say much. The business of tasting wine is just that, business. You're there to taste, not to drink. So . . .

• Remember: You are introspective by nature and distracted by the very aromas around you.

• Take the small amount of wine offered; listen intently to any information given about the wine.

• Holding the glass aloft, swirl the wine (just once) around the glass and look at the way it clings to the sides. This is a visual show of the wine's sugar content. The more sugar, the more it sticks to the sides of the glass.

• Take note of the color. You may wish to close one eye, or pull the glass closer, tilting your head slightly. Don't drink yet! This might be a good time for an occasional "hymph"—a show of mild surprise. What your really looking for is a full rich color that is not clouded with deposits caused during the fermentation process. If the color is deep and full, then chances are the taste will be, too. White wines should be the color of pale straw. Red wines should be a lusty ruby red.

- Now closing the eyes swirl again and inhale deeply, then, as if to punctuate the motion, take a small sip from the glass.
- With eyes still closed, roll the wine around your tongue. Remember, all of this should be done with intense concentration.
- When you have gleaned the very soul of the wine from your taste, spit into the colander provided. Yeah, I know—gross, huh? (Oh! First check to make sure there is one.)
- Take a sip of water to cleanse your palette. Now wipe your mouth and remain noncommittal.
- Every so often, inquire as to the year or location of the vineyards. Then nod as if the answer was just as you suspected it would be.
- Pressed for an opinion? Throwing unusual adjectives at wine ("moody," "determined," "energetic") sometimes seems like a surrealistic party game. My vote is that you stick with noncommital words like "complex" or "intriguing."

What You Can Say

If you're not feeling up to any complicated deception, you can always beg off of the wine tasting entirely. Here are some a good way to get out of going to a tasting while at the same time sounding experienced and pleasantly self-deprecating.

"I've found that my palette is just too sensitive to catch the subtle differences after tasting even a few of the wines."

"I'd rather listen to the suggestions of a few knowledgeable friends who have the time to keep up with the lastest vintages."

"I always listen to my buyer who's an absolute genius."

"Rather than hunting down a good wine, for me the fun is finding a good wine by surprise in the company of good friends and a fine meal."

Other memorable wine-related remarks you can deliver:

Hold your glass aloft and say, "Here's to Louis Pasteur, who said, 'Wine is the most healthful and hygienic of all beverages.'"

When looking at a German wine, ask nonchalantly: "Would you know whether there were more than a hundred days of sun before the harvest?" If there have been a hundred days of sun between May and October then it will probably be a good wine. If more than, say about 120 days, it will probably be a great wine.

When You Want to Change the Subject...

...you can always speak longingly about that wonderful Merlot you found that summer in (insert European locale), when you discovered what it was to be alive. Expound from there as your instincts suggest; be prepared to remark that wine always makes you sentimental, take a deep breath, and then launch confidently and maturely into a new topic of conversation.

Words to the Wise

Looking to leave the best possible impression? Avoid, at all costs, remarks like the following: "Hey, *mon ami,* got any of that Mad Dog 20/20?"

Football

It's inescapable—especially on Sundays during the fall, around New Year's Day, and on (you guessed it) Super Bowl Sunday. To those who are unfamiliar with it, football—either the pro or college variety—may seem a daunting, hard-to-follow sport, full of imposing terminology and impenetrable rules. But you don't have to know all the jargon to enjoy the game. Here's the lowdown on what may be America's biggest sporting spectacle—the game of football.

The Straight Scoop

Two teams, each sporting eleven on-field players at a time, take turns trying to move the football toward the opposing goal line by at least ten yards in no more than four tries (downs). No points are awarded for gaining a fresh four chances (a first down) but the team that does so maintains offensive control of the ball, a factor that can take on immense strategic significance.

A team that carries the oblong ball into the end zone is awarded six points for a touchdown; it then tries to boost the score even further by either kicking the ball at short range through the goalposts for an extra point (a pretty sure bet) or trying to move the ball across the goal line again for what's known as a two-point conversion (a lot more difficult).

Another way to score—and one that's usually reserved for situations where one offense has moved fairly deep into enemy territory but run out of downs before scoring a touchdown—is the field goal (worth three points). This time, the kicker tries to kick the ball through the uprights, but he may be a fair distance away from them, depending on how far his team has moved the ball up to that point. You can also score points—two of them—by tackling an offensive player in his own end zone. Such a defensive maneuver is known as a safety. Unlike the other scores, however, scoring a safety means your own offense gets to take over the ball. Usually, when you score, you kick the ball to the other team—that's called the kickoff.

A punt, on the other hand, is a kick that the offense uses to say, "We don't want you to take over possession from where we're playing now—catch the ball and try to run it back." As a general rule, teams punt when they haven't been able to make a first down or get close enough to try to kick a field goal. The other team then takes over the offensive role.

There are a lot of theories about exactly why football has emerged as such a huge phenomenon in the late twentieth century in the United States; my own opinion is that it's one of the greatest television spectacles. The undeniable drama and conflict of a good football game makes for direct, physical confrontation, again and again, with endless possibilities for slow-motion replays and reverse-angle shots. Even a boring game makes perfect visual sense instantly, even to a casual viewer. You can often tell (more or less) what's going on in an instant, which is not always the case with, say, baseball. The game is a fascinating combination of brains and brawn.

Some people say pro football pretty much reflects America, the country that invented it and fell in love with it. The game is highly competitive, fixated on profits, in love with its own hype, gloriously overexposed, highly commercialized, fast-paced, violent, direct, and only as complicated as you want to make it. It's a perfect game for people with short attention spans—a group that, for better or for worse, forms a huge chunk of the viewing populace.

What You Can Say

Here are a few choice observations to consider including in your discussion of football. I'll leave the focus on the pro game, as it's the one you're most likely to hear about. (There are, be forewarned, plenty of college football enthusiasts out there. Fortunately, most of them keep track of the National Football League, too.)

"I'm having a rough year—I'm a [blank] fan." (Here, you should insert the name of the team having the worst year in the league. Yes, you'll have to check the sports pages for this. It will be worth it. You'll establish yourself as a person who has some knowledge of current standings, but you'll also avoid launching any variation of Who's Going to Make the Playoffs This Year, a subject that sometimes appears to require an advanced degree in calculus to talk about definitively. You may also inspire a little sympathy on the part of your conversational partner. Hey—it's shameless, but it works.)

"Most Super Bowls are just excuses to get together with friends to watch interesting commercials—the games themselves are usually so one-sided that there's not much point in sticking around past halftime." (This is a near-universal complaint among fans. You should be aware, however, that there are a few exceptions to the boring Super Bowl rule. In Super Bowl XX11, the 49ers clipped the Bengals on a great drive led by quarterback Joe Montana, and in Super Bowl XXV, the New York Giants withstood a last-minute attempt from the Bills to kick a gamewinning field goal. Pretty much everything else over the last decade and a half, though, has been a snooze job.)

"Let's face it—the NFC teams have won lots of Super Bowls because they generally play a more physical game, they've got someone who can run the ball, and they know how to stop the run on defense. The NFC champions have usually been the more balanced team in the Super Bowl. AFC squads (with the recent exception of the Denver Broncos), usually have a name quarterback like Drew Bledsoe or Jim Kelly—and not a lot else." (The National Football League is divided into two conferences, American and National. As of this writing, NFC teams have won fourteen of the past sixteen Super Bowls. The rant above is as good an explanation as any for the phenomenon.)

When You Want to Change the Subject...

Wonder aloud how CBS managed to lose the right to broadcast NFL games to the Fox network. You'll then be in a position to take on a discussion of the excesses and oversights of mainstream media giants, and if that's not a topic ripe for examination, I don't know what is.

Words to the Wise

Don't use technical terminology (nickel defense, shallow cross, open side, closed side, etc.) unless you're willing to discuss them in detail. Even fans of long standing sometimes don't know what this stuff actually refers to—if you try to bluff your way through the discussion by mentioning stuff you heard on television, you may start an awkward round of strained silences, mutual nodding, and earnest throat-clearing. (By the way, the nickel defense involves bringing in an extra defensive back—and getting rid of either one defensive lineman or a linebacker—to better protect against an expected pass.)

HOW TO IMPRESS ANYBODY ABOUT

Gems

When people dress up they often adorn themselves with their most impressive jewelry. That's a perfect opportunity to bring the subject of gems up yourself. Wouldn't it be great if you could say something like "My, what a lovely sapphire that is...it's Sri Lankan, isn't it?"

The Straight Scoop

Stones are usually worn today for one of three reasons: The wearer wants to show off the value of the stone, he or she just thinks the piece looks cool, or he or she goes in for all that New Age health-improvement business.

As late as the eighteenth century many learned people believed that ingesting powdered gems could cure them of a variety of ills. Topaz supposedly cured asthma. Jet made even a bad toothache go away, amber would take care of that nasty goiter, amethyst would neutralize poison, and a sapphire would cure insanity. Of course these didn't work, but at least the treatments proved that someone cared enough to try to heal you with the very best.

Then of course there's the notion of cursed gems. Everybody's heard of the Hope Diamond, the 112-carat steel-blue megastar of the gem world—and its long history of bad luck. But then the everyday opal can provide plenty of bad luck for the hapless wearer who's unknowingly appropriating someone else's birthstone. According to the legend, if you're not born in October, it's seriously bad luck to wear opals.

Not all stones are what they appear. In this age of cubic zirconium (CZ for short), the actual value of anything anyone wears can be, um ... unclear. That may work to your advantage.

CZs abound on the market, as do man-made rubies and sapphires and irradiated gems. (Irradiation: when a stone is basically cooked until it changes color.) With this procedure a white diamond can be changed into any number of colors, including yellow, forest green, pink, and chocolate brown. These colors can be found naturally in diamonds but their value (when found in a natural stone) is quite a bit higher. Only a certified gemologist can tell the difference between a naturally occurring tone and an irradiated one.

A filled stone is one that has been repaired, perhaps because the stone (usually one of the softer ones like emerald) has scratches or cracks. It is filled with powdered paste of the same type of stone being repaired. So it could be argued that the original stone is simply being repaired with a substance of equal value. So, what is the harm? Well, many argue that a misconception is being put forth; if people aren't informed about what they're buying, a misconception that can lead to mistrust between the seller and the buyer. The gem industry relies on trust among all parties involved. Once a seller's reputation becomes tarnished (as it were) she might as well pack up her spyglass and move to another town.

The bottom line: Lots of fake stuff looks really, really convincing these days. If you're buying, get a professional to look something over. If you're complimenting, just assume that what the person is trying to pass off is genuine.

What You Can Say

"You didn't go all the way to Japan for those beautiful pearls, did you?" (Cultured pearls are found today in huge oyster beds farmed off the coast of Japan. They are harvested when the oyster has been given enough time to build the pearl around an irritant such as a pebble or grain of sand.)

"Don't keep that necklace in the drawer—wearing pearls is good for them." (The oils on your skin really do condition the pearls. Don't wear them in the shower, though—that's likely to damage the surface.)

"I envy people born in April...imagine getting diamonds for every birthday." (Diamonds are the birthstone for those born in April. A basic familiarity with the months attached to the various stones will go a long way toward helping you impress others. The remaining months, and their stones: January—garnet; February—amethyst; March—bloodstone or aquamarine; May—emerald; June—pearl or moonstone; July—ruby; August—sardonyx or peridot; September—sapphire; October—opal or tourmaline; November—topaz; December—turquoise or lapis lazuli.)

"A true Alexandrite will change its color." Alexandrites were named for Alexander II of Russia, where they are often found. Synthetic versions are common in Korea; both will change color when exposed to natural light (purple), or artificial light (blue-gray). True Alexandrite are very rare. The bigger and more vibrant it is, the greater the chance it is synthetic.

"That emerald is amazing. It's the deepest green I've ever seen." (The deeper the green, the higher the value of the emerald.)

When You Want to Change the Subject...

Be prepared to ask about the country of origin of the stone in question. Once you've done that, it should be a fairly easy matter to transfer the topic of conversation over to the customs, politics, or recent events in that part of the world—or, if your geography is a little rusty, to the social functions that adornments like jewels and clothes play in various communities.

Words to the Wise

Trying to get away with wearing a synthetic diamond? You'll probably need to polish your rhetorical skills...and do a little intelligent preparation. Don't wear a fake diamond that is too large or too small. About half a carat in size is usually a good balance between the fake stone and the fake gold surrounding it. You can try for a bigger stone, but you're going to need a great deal of confidence—and a six-prong setting, rather than the suspicious-looking four prongs—to pull this off.

Whatever the size of the "diamond" you wear, be prepared to ignore the stares and act as though nothing's amiss. She who hesitates is lost. When someone mentions the stone (which is likely), act a bit embarrassed and say, "Oh these—Grandma insisted I have them. I used the feel a little silly owning them. I almost never go anywhere where I have a reason to show them off. But then one day I said darn it, if one can't wear jewels to the grocery store, one shouldn't own them. After all, Grandma would have."

HOW TO IMPRESS ANYBODY ABOUT

Golf

There must be something very special about the game of golf. If you're like me, you've probably seen people out on the greens at 7:30 A.M. in the freezing rain and sleet, grabbing a quick nine holes before they go to the office. The question is: What do golf enthusiasts know that the rest of us don't?

If you ask them, the regular players will give you vague explanations that emphasize the Zen-like tranquility of the sport, its complex physics, the way the whole undertaking has of looking like a ballet of the unpredictable, the way it posits forces of nature against the mind, etcetera. In other words, golf people feel as strongly about their sport as baseball people feel about theirs. Except golf people actually play the game.

Suppose you've been invited to the course, and you don't know your three wood from your putter. Have no fear—grab your argyles. I'll walk you through this.

The Straight Scoop

You're probably already familiar with some of the basics. The game is played on a course with a small white ball and clubs with wood and steel heads. One hits the small ball with the appropriate club so that the ball will eventually roll with a pleasant kerplunk into a hole dug into the ground that holds a cup. The fewer times you have to hit the ball to hear the kerplunk the better you're doing. This hit-until-kerplunk process is repeated either nine or eighteen times.

Sad but true department: In many settings, golf is going to cost you. Greens fees (the cost of using the course) run from about $25 at a municipal course to over $1,000 just outside of Tokyo. Status can be a big issue in golf; you may be judged by the equipment you bring along. A set of clubs can cost from about $300 for the low-end store brands to many thousands for a custom-made set. A good golf bag is available for something like $100 and up, shoes cost $50 and up, and a glove runs upwards of $20. You get the picture.

Buying clubs? You really don't have to. You can rent them for around $10 to $15. A full set of clubs may impress your companions, but it is not necessary. What is necessary is that you know what to call them. A full set has drivers (also known as woods) from 1 through 5; irons, from 1 to 9; a pitching wedge; a sand wedge; a putter or two; an umbrella; and a telescoping ball grabber for water hazards. The lower the number, the longer the handle and the flatter the face on the club. If the ball you're hitting has a long way to go, you'll want a club with a low number. If you're interested in placement and precision, go for one with a higher number. Tournament play allows only fourteen clubs in the bag, but any golfer can hold his head up high with six basic clubs (called a half set), and three specialty clubs.

Are lessons worth paying for? Well, the best way to answer that question is to observe that bad habits learned early in golf are devilishly hard to break. (Just about any experienced golfer will attest to this.) You may decide to pick up some book that claims to help you improve your game, but most experts agree that writing about how to actually hit a golf ball is pretty much an exercise in futility. It would probably serve you better to spend a day or two at the driving range with a friend who knows how.

What You Can Say

"One more triple bogey and I'm calling it a day." (Finishing the hole with the same number of shots as the par rating is, of course, called par. One shot more than par is a bogey, two shots over is a double bogey, three over is a triple bogey, after that you just say "I got a four" or five, etc.)

"That woman just finished with a double eagle, she should go pro." (One shot under par is called a birdie, two shots under is an eagle, and three under is a double eagle.)

"You got the best score on the last hole, you're up first." (The better player tees off first, the corollary being that the player with the lowest score on the last hole goes first off the next tee. This rule is overcome if the rightful first hitter offers to let you go first.)

"Fore!" (A warning cry to anyone in the way of a shot. Most players save it for times when they can tell a recently smacked ball is headed in a bad direction and likely to hit someone. Instead of hollering "Fore!" before you swing, wait and make sure no one's ahead of you and likely to get beaned. At the most you should wave politely to the group up ahead.)

"I think of golf as being like a game of chess." (You need to think two or three moves ahead every time you hit the ball in order to make your next shot as easy as possible.)

"I like to follow short game guru Phil Rodgers's tip on chipping: using a putting stroke with a lofted club." (The most important part of chipping is the setup. You need to create the right position right from the start of the swing.)

"As Kevin Costner says, '... there is no feeling like a well-struck golf shot.'" (Many of the game's passionate adherents agree.)

"Golf is a great excuse for drinking beer in the morning." (Golf is one of the only games in which a morning brew is a typical part of the proceedings.)

When You Want To Change the Subject...

"The big question the whole Tiger Woods phenomenon raises for me is..." (Here insert any pertinent query you feel comfortable addressing. For example, have massive endorsement deals changed the cultural landscape for better or worse? Does a single racial designation do any of us justice as Americans? Should sports dreams play as large a role as they do for kids today? Is there such a thing as media overkill? How on earth does someone get a first name like Tiger?)

Words to the Wise

Take some lessons before you invest in any equipment; rent first, and ask your spouse or significant other how he or she feels about your taking up this sport. Watch that wardrobe. Don't drink and drive (golf balls). Last but not least: That stuff they say about golfers getting hit by lightning during storms is true. When the skies get dark and ugly, it's time to head inside.

Great Quotes and Speeches

One of the best ways to sound smarter than you are and impress others with your acumen is to be able to recite, at a moment's notice, the words of people who really *were* smarter than you are. Hard to believe, I know, but people used to do this sort of thing all the time. When the opportunity presented itself during dinner or another gathering, and a crowd gathered expectantly, awaiting some kind of divine wisdom (or at least a good joke), nobody went away disappointed.

The Straight Scoop

Here are some fine examples of sharp stuff someone wrote or said in years gone by. Pick a few that light your fire, invest some time and commit the quotes to memory. That way, the next time you're stuck for a sharp comeback, or someone asks you to hold forth at a public gathering, or you're asked to identify a famous quote that has inspired you, you'll be able to do something other than stare blankly at your shoetops.

What You Can Say

Politics and History

Civilization is a moment and not a condition, a voyage and not a harbor. (Historian Arnold Toynbee's definition of civilization, *Reader's Digest,* October 1955)

There is no instance of a country having benefited from prolonged warfare. Hence to fight and conquer in all our battles is not supreme excellence; supreme excellence consists in breaking the enemy's resistance without fighting. (Sun Tzu)

On the day of victory no one is tired. (Arab proverb)

Men willingly believe what they wish. (Julius Caesar)

The government is the only known vessel that leaks from the top. (James Reston)

Now and then, an innocent man is sent to the legislature. (Kin Hubbard)

Government is like a big baby—an alimentary canal with a big appetite at one end and no responsibility at the other end. (Ronald Reagan)

The form of government that is most suitable to the artist is no government at all. (Oscar Wilde)

Nature

In wilderness is the preservation of the world. (Henry David Thoreau)

To the artist there is never anything ugly in nature. (Auguste Rodin)

Nature never breaks her own laws. (Leonardo da Vinci)

Fortune and Destiny

Fortune gives too much to many, enough to none. (Martial)

To be thrown upon one's own resources is to be cast into the very lap of fortune, for our faculties then undergo a development and display an enemy of which they were previously unsusceptible. (Benjamin Franklin)

Time is the most valuable thing a man can spend. (Theophrastus)

Our greatest thoughts come from the heart. (Luc de Clapiers)

Nothing is impossible to a willing heart. (John Heywood)

Delays have dangerous ends. (William Shakespeare)

Spirituality and Religion

The road to Hades is easy to travel. (Bion)

God helps those that help themselves. (Benjamin Franklin)

The goal of life is living in agreement with nature. (Zeno)

As to thinking, hold to that which is simple. (Lao-Tzu's *Advice on Right Living*)

The Christian life is not a way *out* but a way *through* life. (Reverend Billy Graham)

The only complete love is love for God. (George Harrison)

Social Commentary

TV is chewing gum for the eyes. (Frank Lloyd Wright)

Along with responsible newspapers, we must have responsible readers. (Arthur Sulzberger)

Necessity has no law. (Saint Augustine)

If you find an error, please understand that we put it there on purpose. We try to publish something for everyone, and some people are always looking for something to criticize. (Famous—and perhaps mythical—notice from an exasperated newspaper editor to his readers.)

Conflict and Survival

Never fight fair with a stranger, boy. You'll never get out of the jungle that way. (Arthur Miller)

Float like a butterfly, sting like a bee. (Muhammad Ali)

Disobedience, in the eyes of anyone who has read history, is man's original virtue. It is through disobedience that progress has been made, through disobedience and rebellion. (Oscar Wilde)

The Neglected Art of Making It Through the Day Happily

To laugh is proper to man. (François Rabelais)

Let every man mind his own business. (Miguel de Cervantes)

> If on my theme I rightly think,
> There are five reasons why I drink—
> Good wine, a friend, because I'm dry,
> Or lest I should be by and by,
> Or any other reason why.
> (Henry Aldrich)

Pain is short, and joy is eternal. (Johann Christoph Friedrich von Schiller)

Human affairs are like a chess game: Only those who do not take it seriously can be called good players. (Hung Tzu'cheng)

When You Want to Change the Subject...

You should be ready with some explanation of what inspired you to memorize the quote, or why it's significant to you. This explanation can allow you to point the conversation in just about any direction— say, the priorities of the educational system, or the memories of childhood.

Words to the Wise

Beware of monopolizing the proceedings. This maneuver works best when you're acting to fill in an awkward blank spot, or when you can point to a single, strong parallel between the meaning of the quote you've memorized and a recent topic of conversation. Spouting lots of quotes, without any regard for the context of the discussion, is a great way to earn a reputation as a blowhard and will impress no one.

The History of the Earth and Human Evolution

How recent are human beings? Compared to, you know, dinosaurs? When did forests start? And, while we're pondering the evolutionary timescape, which came first, the chicken or the egg?

Let's take that oft-cited last question first—because it does have a correct, surprisingly common sense answer. The egg came first. Why? Because chickens, like everything else that is alive, evolve. So imagine if you will, Chicken Number One. The first chicken off the evolutionary assembly line—the first chicken worthy of being called a chicken—came from *somewhere,* right? It evolved from a pre-chicken form of some kind—a form that, like it or not, had essentially the same reproductive system as Chicken Number One. That means Chicken Number One sprang from an egg, even though its mom wouldn't have qualified as a chicken, but as a pre-chicken. I don't know about you, but that's a load off of *my* mind.

Now that we've cleared up one of life's most popular enduring mysteries, let's move on to the main question—*what evolved when?* Which creatures came first ... in the fundamental sense? And *when* did they come first? If you're only interested in chickens, stop here—they (along with other modern birds) appear to have shown up somewhere between 65 million and 200 million years ago—undomesticated, that is. If you're interested in other arrivals to the planetary party, and in the geological events that made the whole shindig possible, read on.

The Straight Scoop

Let's go back—way back—to the *really* old days, some 4.6 billion years ago. You're stuck in the *Precambrian Era,* a four billion-year interval that scientists believe saw the beginnings of life as we know it. High points of the period: bacterial cells, algae, and fungi.

Eventually, marine invertebrates showed up. But there was this nice, long stretch of ... algae primacy. Algae may seem boring to us nowadays, but it had the prime spot on earth for quite a while. We tend to lose sight of that these days. (And, via photosynthesis, blue-green algae *still* produces most of the world's oxygen.)

Fast-forward to the beginning of the Paleozoic Era—which began 570 million years ago and is often referred to as the Era of Ancient Life. Compared to the Precambrian Era, life practically jitterbugs its way across the global stage during the Paleozoic era. Terrestrial plants show up perhaps 500 million years ago; they settle in for good around 410 million years ago. The first fish start to make their way through ancient oceans 500 million years ago; amphibians show up around 410 million years ago. By the turn of the Paleozoic Era, 285 million years ago, insects you and I would recognize have shown up, as have some reptiles, some of which have a distinctly mammal-like appearance.

The tempo picks up briskly in the Mesozoic Era, which lasts for a mere 130 million years. During this stretch of time, known as the Age of Reptiles, dinosaurs take the stage in a world whose plant life is best described as heavy on the ferns. Thanks to a certain Hollywood blockbuster, just about everyone nods sagely nowadays when informed that one of the three periods during this era is known as Jurassic. It's the one in the middle. Before the Jurassic period, when the dinosaurs first showed up, there's the Triassic period. After the Jurassic period comes the Cretaceous period, notable for the spread—and extinction—of the dinosaurs, and for the appearance of primitive mammals. Birds you and I might consider familiar also show up during the Cretaceous period.

After the Age of Reptiles comes the Age of Mammals. Finally! Our turn, right? Well, not quite. It takes another hundred million years or so—give or take a couple of hundred millennia—for apes to evolve. That's about 38 million years ago, about the same period when forests started to spread. It's another 32 million years before the earliest known human-like primates make their appearance. Hominids (early humans) show up for the Old Stone Age—ah, those happy days of yesteryear—which started about 3.5 million years ago. Large carnivores abound; then a series of four Ice Ages kicks in during the Quaternary period, and vast numbers of mammals are wiped out. Not our ancestors, though.

After the ice ages come and go, we reach the narrowest, and most recent, sliver of geologic time—the time of modern human dominance. Finally.

So—how long has *homo sapiens* actually ruled the roost? How long can we flatter ourselves as having occupied the top of a pop chart of our very own invention? In the grand evolutionary scheme of things, we've been the dominant species for hardly an instant. The Holocene epoch of the Quaternary period of the Cenozoic Era—or, to put it another way, the period that includes now—encompasses only ten thousand years.

That's our slice. Ten thousand years. From cave paintings to Homer to Confucius to Shakespeare to instant e-mail retrieval ... it all fits into a tiny line on the furthest right-hand corner of the timeline, a line you'd probably have to have pointed out to you unless you knew you were supposed to look for it, one you probably couldn't foresee without the aid of a magnifying glass.

What You Can Say

"Human beings tend to forget that they're pretty recent arrivals on the scene." As we've seen, the whole story started—we think—something like 4.6 billion years ago. That means all of human evolution and culture takes place within a segment of time that represents an almost incalculably tiny fraction of the total. Short message: We showed up well after the party got started. The next time you're feeling superior while strolling through the zoo, watching a nature documentary, or swatting some pesky (but evolutionarily road tested) mosquito, remember—we're the new kids on the block.

"Charles Darwin wasn't the first to theorize about evolutionary processes." Certain evolutionary concepts popped up in the work of some of the ancient Greeks, including Thales, Empedocles, Anaximander, and Aristotle. Others who put forward important ideas in this area included a French naturalist named Jean Lamarck. During the many centuries of social and scientific dominance by the Christian church, however, inquiry into evolutionary theory was rigidly suppressed in favor of a literal interpretation of the early passages of the book of Genesis. Remarkably, Darwin's evolutionary research and theories—providing, at long last, a coherent theory of evolution— emerged at virtually the same time as that of another English scientist, Alfred Russell Wallace. Wallace was working independently on a paper that's basic theory was almost identical to Darwin's. He submitted his manuscript to Darwin in order to obtain his insights— just as Darwin was revising *The Origin of Species,* on which he had been working for at least sixteen years! (The two made a joint presentation to a scientific group incorporating both Wallace's paper and an outline of Darwin's forthcoming book.)

"People forget that it wasn't Darwin who coined the phrase 'survival of the fittest.' It was Herbert Spencer—a British sociologist. The idea is that organisms that have failed to effectively adapt to their environment are at a comparative disadvantage to organisms that *have* adapted successfully. Members of the former group die, and their line dwindles or vanishes entirely; members of the latter group live to reproduce.

When You Want to Change the Subject …

… point out that Darwin's book *The Origin of Species* is one of the most influential volumes ever published (although it was a while before its extraordinary impact was felt). Ask your conversational partners to identify their nominees for similarly earthshaking books. The Bible? *Quotations from Chairman Mao? Valley of the Dolls?* The possibilities are endless.

Words to the Wise

Every once in a while, you'll run into someone who insists that the world is only a few thousand years old, and that the sociologically and artistically masterful creation myths appearing in the Book of Genesis are meant to withstand scientific scrutiny. This person probably has very strong opinions, so don't try to a) change his or her mind by appealing to current scientific research or b) make fun of the person's belief system. Smile, nod, mention how "fascinating" the person's theories are, and move on to a subject that both of you can address intelligently. Like the weather.

HOW TO IMPRESS ANYBODY ABOUT

Homer's Odyssey

The Odyssey is one of the oldest works of Western literature. (Others in this particular "oldies but goodies" category include *The Odyssey*'s companion piece, *The Iliad*, and the Bible.) *The Odyssey* is also one of the most influential literary creations of all time.

In ancient times, the poem's companion piece, *The Iliad*, was considered the more significant of the two works. One current strain of scholarship argues that the two poems were created by different authors. The styles are certainly quite different; where *The Iliad* shows unity, a careful progression, a tight focus, and a certain militarism, *The Odyssey* offers complexity, variety, and consistent fascination with questions of family and individual identity. Both poems appear to be rooted in oral composition. For the sake of simplicity, though, I'm going to assume, from this point forward, that there was a single author named Homer who wrote the pieces that have been historically associated with him.

For the last few centuries, it's *The Odyssey* that has most captivated readers. It may be a bit of an overstatement to describe *The Odyssey* as the single work now most likely to be classified as the sublime literary achievement of the ancient world, but it's probably not *that* much of an overstatement. In any event, you should probably have a basic idea of what goes on in this story, as it's frequently cited as the precursor to just about everything of importance in Western litera-ture—especially the modern novel. (A currently popular paperback edition of *The Odyssey* identifies it as "the true ancestor of the long live of novels that have followed it.")

So what's it all about?

The Straight Scoop

The Odyssey is an epic poem—initially meant to be sung—completed in about the eighth century B.C. It relates, in a form of ancient Greek, the adventures of the warrior Odysseus as he seeks to return from the Trojan Wars to his island kingdom of Ithaca. (In Latin, Odysseus's name is rendered as Ulysses.) It was once believed that the Trojan Wars, and Odysseus's subsequent adventures, took place shortly after 1200 B.C.

The hero of this extraordinary adventure is by turns shrewd, brave, calculating, and a little distant. He's a survivor, first and foremost—and some of the people who share adventures with him have a tendency to suffer fates similar to that of the anonymous, interchangeable, soon-to-be-obliterated guys in red shirts who beam down with Kirk, Spock, and McCoy to explore strange new worlds in the original *Star Trek*. Odysseus, the king of Ithaca, has no phasers or dilithium crystals to fall back on, however. This long-suffering hero must rely on his righteousness, his wits, and his unfailing bravery in order to return to his wife and son. It takes a while—okay, a *long* while—but the family is reunited.

The story has two strands. Odysseus, detained by the sea god Poseidon, has been unable to make his way back to Ithaca to reclaim his throne and reunite his family. Telemachus, inspired by the disguised goddess Athena (who is friendly to the family's plight), stands up to the suitors who are sponging off the estate of his father in the hope of marrying his faithful, ever-patient wife Penelope. The young prince sets off in search of Odysseus, eventually learning that his father was held prisoner by the nymph Calypso. Odysseus ceaselessly tries to make his way home; Telemachus tries to pin down his father's fate and whereabouts. The two are ultimately united on the island of Ithaca, thanks in no small part to the guiding influence of the sympathetic goddess Athena. Disguised as a beggar, Odysseus develops a strategy that allows him and his son to retake the palace, slaughter all the suitors, and restore the long-divided family. It works. After years of ignorance of her husband's fate, the faithful Penelope is reunited with Odysseus.

That's the main thrust of the tale—but no short summary can give you an idea of the extraordinary depth of character and incident that Odysseus, Telemachus, and Penelope encounter in the *Odyssey*. Here's a short summary of some of the memorable supporting characters in Homer's epic poem, which will be enough to get you through the conversation in impressive fashion:

Athena: The goddess of wisdom, and the primary ally of Odysseus as he makes his way home through a complex, seemingly over-whelming series of challenges. At key points in the story, she emerges to offer Odysseus or Telemachus important advice on how to proceed. Her initial encounters with Telemachus inspire him to go to sea to learn his father's fate.

The Suitors: A big, crass gathering of loudmouthed layabouts, they've taken up residence in the palance at Ithaca. They're intent on either devouring the absent Odysseus's wealth or forcing his wife Penelope to decide which of them she will marry. She's been playing delaying games for years, refusing to either accept or reject any suitor's overture. (She explains that she cannot marry until she finishes a shroud for Odysseus; at night, she secretly undoes her weaving.) The two leaders among the suitors—and presumably rejects of the Miss Manners Correspondence Program of the Ancient World—are the arrogant and insolent Antinoos and Eurymachus. Guess which two suitors die first when Odysseus makes it back home?

Laertes: Odysseus's old father—seasoned, if past his prime, he is nevertheless a daunting warrior. The fact that Odysseus has failed to return from the war is so deeply demoralizing to him that he fails to venture into the city of Ithaca, but by the story's end he sees his son once again and rejoices.

Anticleia: Odysseus's mother, who dies of sorrow during his absence from Ithaca. He encounters her as a shade, but cannot touch her.

Eumaeus: A faithful servant of Odysseus who treats the disguised king kindly, despite his humble appearance upon his return to Ithaca. In return for his good works and his assistance in overcoming the suitors, Odysseus grants him lands and a title near the poem's conclusion.

Eurycleia: She served as Odysseus's nurse when he was a child; she remains faithful to his memory, and recognizes him (thanks to a scar on his leg) when he returns to Ithaca in the guise of a beggar. Odysseus swears her to silence.

Philoetius: A goatherd—and, with Eurycleia and Eumaeus, one of only three servants in Odysseus's household to remain loyal to him. He closes the doors of the courtyard, trapping the suitors.

Menelaus: If it weren't for his marital problems, the Trojan Wars would never have taken place at all, and Odysseus would have been spared a whole lot of trouble. Menelaus is a superb warrior of great bravery who fought with Odysseus in Troy. Reunited with his own wife, Helen (she whose face launched a thousand ships), he is a generous host to Telemachus, and offers the son of Odysseus guidance, information, and moral support.

Nestor: An old, garrulous comrade in arms of Odysseus. Telemachus goes to meet with him on Argos in the hope of learning more about his father.

Calypso: A nymph, in love with Odysseus, who refuses to let him leave her island. He spends seven years with her.

Circe: A sorceress; her potion leaves Odysseus's men in the form of pigs. Odysseus threatens Circe, then "tastes her favors" (in the euphemism favored by my old classics teacher), and convinces her to restore his men to their original form. She lets them leave—but only after watching over Odysseus and his men for a year, and then offering counsel on the best way for them to make it back to Ithaca.

Alcinoos: King of the Phaeacians. An extremely generous host to Odysseus; he listens to accounts of the remarkable adventures the wanderer has passed, then provides the means for Odysseus's long-delayed return to Ithaca.

Arete: Queen of the Phaeacians. (The name means "virtue" in Greek.)

Nausicaa: Daughter of Alcinoos and Arete. Finds Odysseus on the shore of her country after his long sea wanderings, and helps him to connect with her parents, the king and queen.

Polyphemus: Polyphemus is of the race known as Cyclops. More to the point, though, he's the son of Poseidon, which means big trouble for our hero. Why? Well, Odysseus managed to escape the fiend's cave after he used a sharp stick to put the brute's eye out, thanks to some cunning trickery. The attack certainly seemed justified—after all, Polyphemus had devoured four of Odysseus's men—but it earned our hero the wrath of Poseidon. That made getting back to Ithaca a tricky proposition.

Poseidon: The sea god, and father to Polyphemus. If you're a big god, you get to torment mortals who don't show you the proper respect. (And Odysseus doesn't—he not only blinds the blood-thirsty Polyphemus, but he also taunts him as he heads for the horizon on his ship.) Accordingly, Poseidon makes it his business to frustrate Odysseus's every attempt to return home, and is a factor in the destruction of many of his men. Rule for survival: Try not to serve under a commander who's angered a powerful god. (If it weren't for Athena's speaking to Zeus on Odysseus's behalf, Poseidon would have simply destroyed Odysseus. But then there wouldn't have been much of a story.)

Eurylachus: Odysseus's lieutenant, who (unwisely) gets into disputes with his superior on several occasions. Eurylachus and his men are foolish enough to slaughter and consume the cattle of Helios, thus infuriating Zeus. They die as a result.

Teiresias: Skilled prophet whom Odysseus encounters in the land of the dead. He offers the Ithacan king detailed advice on the best way to make it home to Ithaca—and on how to patch up relations with Poseidon once things settle down. By following Teiresias's advice—which involves yet another journey, and an offering to Poseidon after certain signs appear in a foreign land—Odysseus is promised a happy and secure old age at home: "After that I was to go back home and make ceremonial sacrifices to the everlasting gods who live in the far-flung heavens... he said that Death would come to me in his gentlest form out of the sea, and that when he took me I should be worn out after an easy old age and surrounded by a prosperous folk." After Penelope agrees to this plan, the three generations of warriors—Laertes, Odysseus, and Telemachus— unite to vanquish the vengeful families of the suitors. Odysseus is at long last set on a course that promises peace and stability, although some of Teiresias's instructions must still be faithfully carried out before the king of Ithaca's long stretch of difficulty is truly concluded.

What You Can Say

"Do you think Homer really existed?" The best answer scholarship has been able to come up with: maybe, maybe not. Scholars still aren't entirely sure whether the author of *The Odyssey* was a single person (according to legend, a blind minstrel), a committee, or some intriguing, complex combination of the two. Scholars *are* pretty certain that this poem arose from earlier legendary accounts, however, and was reworked into its present form—either by one person or a group—to yield one of the great stories of all time. That reputation has persisted for centuries.

"In the end, the whole authorship dispute is a little like the anti-Stratfordian arguments against Shakespeare, isn't it? Whatever the truth behind the development of *The Odyssey*, we're still left with a sublime work of art." If you're feeling brave, you can even mention the character of Demodocos. He's a blind minstrel who sings the story of the Trojan horse for Odysseus and his royal hosts, Arete and Alcinoos—as well as other members of the court. Some scholars feel this character may be meant to represent Homer.

"For my part, I prefer the Penguin translation by E. V. Rieu, because it doesn't even attempt to render the text in verse." Prose-translation adherents (of which I'm one) often argue that the effort to recreate rhymes and rhythms within the poem are needlessly distracting and distancing to modern readers. There have been countless eminent prose and verse translations of *The Odyssey* over the years. Among the most prominent prose efforts are those of Rieu (whose version is quoted in this article) and Andrew Lang. Perhaps the most important (and accessible) verse translation is Richmond Lattimore's

When You Want to Change the Subject...

...just point out that Odysseus is the basic prototype of more (and more varied) long-suffering, adventuresome protagonists than you can shake a stick at, from Hamlet to Alice in Wonderland to Leopold Bloom...and there are countless others. That gives you plenty of room to maneuver. Steer the conversation to Shakespeare, Lewis Carroll, or (for the truly adventurous), James Joyce, who took Homer's poem as the model for his masterpiece *Ulysses*.

Words to the Wise

The Odyssey is such a superb piece of writing that, given a good translation, you'll probably end up devouring it in a week or so without meaning to. Give this masterpiece half a chance, and you won't regret having done so. Keep it on your night table and leaf through it until you find a passage you like (which won't take long). Pretty soon you'll be hooked, and then you won't have to fake anything.

Horses

Horses need a home of their own, one that's warm and tight. They need plenty of food, blankets, expensive leather accessories, and they absolutely insist on being taken out every day. Let's face it, horses live better than a lot of people do. But owning a "quality" horse does prove two things beyond a shadow of a doubt: that you have an eye for good horse flesh, and that you have the requisite heaps of cash necessary to maintain the animal.

Suppose you don't own a horse, though. Suppose you don't even know how to ride. And suppose you still want to appear knowledgeable about the subject, but horses, to be quite frank, scare you a little.

Fear is actually a pretty good companion to the beginning horseman; fear of the animal, and respect for it, sometimes go hand in hand. And every honest rider will admit to having known a horse or two that was a bit intimidating.

Even if you never actually get on a horse, you'll be able to participate in a meaningful conversation about them—and hold your own during the obligatory walk through the stables—by reading the short summary below.

The Straight Scoop

A horse that is broken in (or just "broke" if you're hanging with cowboys) has already been trained; it knows what to do. A broken-in horse will respond positively to a calm voice, a gentle touch, a cube of sugar, or a carrot.

A horse can see out of each eye separately. (Their eyes also magnify objects.) The horse is trained to be approached and mounted from the left. So walking head on into the horse's face will not be your best move. Stay on the left side, talk in a calm voice, and keep your movements slow and confident. If all else fails, try clucking. It's not quite as hip, but it will get the horse's attention.

Your first test of bravery comes when the horse wants you to pass along some grub. Don't worry; the horse knows that the food will taste better than your fingers. The only way it's going to bite you is if you put your fingers in the way of the snack. That's easy enough to avoid: hold the snack in the middle of the palm of your hand. Your palm will be soft, slightly cupped, with the fingers together. The horse will then move its massive head toward the offering, sniffing and slobbering until it gets a sense of the size of what's being offered, and thinking about whether or not it's worth the effort. Stay relaxed; keep your hand cupped so that animal won't knock the apple from your hand—that would make you look skittish and it would just plain frustrate the horse. If you do your part the horse will take the apple in one bite and stand there in front of you to eat it.

Reach for the horse's halter (the headpiece that rests over the horse's brow and nose) at the side of the head. Keep talking to the horse in the same calm, controlled voice. Gently pull the horse toward your chest. Scratch it behind the ear and then move to the wide place between its eyes. Rub briskly up and down. Then gently pet the soft part between its nostrils gently. If the horse is not wearing a halter, then you probably shouldn't reach for it. Instead, slowly and smoothly reach up and scratch behind the ear. Most animals, just like us humans, love to be scratched in places they can't quite reach.

Remember to approach the horse from the left side and keep your hand calmly moving along its body as you move. Always let the horse know where you are. Stay away from positions directly behind the horse. If you must walk behind it, pat its hindquarters like you'd pat a friend on the back and move smoothly around to the other flank.

Keep your body close to the horse. The closer you are, the better the chance you'll just get shoved if the horse gets frisky. Moving too far away gives the horse the chance to really wind up on you. Do keep an eye on those legs because some of the more nervous horses are kickers. Be especially watchful if you spot a red ribbon tied to the tail. This means the horse is a known kicker, and you're well advised to stay away from the hindquarters region altogether. Interested in actually learning how to ride the thing? There are two time-tested strategies: 1) Climb in the saddle and hope for the best, or 2) pay someone who knows how to teach you. Although plenty of people have gotten good results from 1), I'd strongly suggest you opt for 2).

What You Can Say

Here's some more terminology and background information to toss in at appropriate points of the discussion when you're trying to impress the horse crowd.

"Now there's a regal beast." (I suggest that you start out by calling the horse gender-neutral names like Baby, Beauty, and so on. That is because I'm assuming you may not know whether you're looking at a stallion [adult male], a gelding [a stallion that has been castrated], or a mare [a female of breeding age]. A newborn of either sex is a foal. A male horse from weaning to four years is called a colt, and a female from weaning to four years is called a filly. A baby one to two years old of either sex is a yearling. An older female horse is called a nag.)

"He reminds me of my first horse, Taffy. He first blooded me when I was seven. God, I loved that horse." (If you see a horse that seems out of sorts and kind of, well, frustrated and all alone in a corral, that's most likely a stallion. Me, I'd give him some room. It's not an apple or a pat on the nose he's in the mood for. He's probably not eager to make new friends, either. At least not with you. There's a good chance that the stallion has been put up to stud. If you get a chance to observe the actual process of boy meets girl, be forewarned: It's quite a spectacle. Don't expect poetry and candlelight, though.)

"Mind if I give (horse's name) a little treat?" (A snack can go a long way toward winning over a horse, but remember to ask the owner first. The beast may just be on a special diet. You might want to reach down and grab a good handful of longer weeds and hold it out where the horse can see it. Keep talking and clicking and the horse should come over. If you've really come prepared, you'll pull an apple, a sugar cube, or a handful of grain out of your pocket. All of this stuff is very useful when walking around stables.)

"Our Bernie was an Appaloosa, about sixteen and a half hands tall." (That's from the ground to the shoulder—a convenient fixed point from which to measure. A horse's height is always referred to in terms of hands. One hand equals four inches. So that would make a five feet six inch–tall horse sixteen-and-a-half hands tall. The Appaloosa is a particularly popular animal, of the "hardy breed of riding horses, developed in the North American West, having a mottled hide, vertically striped hoofs, and eyes that show a relatively large proportion of white," according to the folks in the know at Random House. Now you'll be able to pick out a horse that reminds you of that fictional beloved animal from your youth. If you're asked to ride, you may opt to decline politely—because the tender memories of childhood are often best left undisturbed.)

"What's the matter, boy—do you hear bandits over that ridge?" (Said in jest, of course, and to the horse, not your host. The ears of a horse can provide the observant humans with a surprising amount of information about how the horse is feeling at any given moment. The ears rest forward when the horse is relaxed; if it hears something new, it will prick up its ears in the direction of the noise.)

"I remember my grandfather told me once that a horse can only breathe through its nose, no matter how tired it may be." (This is one reason that a horse can become overheated and sweat so profusely.)

"You look like you've been rode hard and put up wet." (This expression is usually meant to describe a rider's scruffy appearance, since no good horseman (or woman) would misuse a horse in this way.

Horses must be meticulously groomed and attended to: walked, rubbed down, washed with tepid water, and dried off after a ride. On a cool night, the horse should get a blanket.)

"I love your pinks—where did you get them?" (Red hunting jackets are called pinks. You have to earn the red jacket and then get invited to wear it by those running the hunt. Everyone else wears black jackets.)

When You Want to Change the Subject...

You may want to make a reference to some of the famous horses in history and mythology:

Bucephalus: Alexander the Great's horse. So wild no one else could ride it.

Byerly Turk: One of the three stallions on which the thoroughbred line of race horses was founded.

Ching Chui: one of the six famous warhorses of the Chinese emperor T'ai Tsung.

Copenhagen: The favorite mount of the Duke of Wellington, which he rode into battle at Waterloo.

Darley Arabian: One of the three stallions on which the thoroughbred line of race horses was founded.

Flicka: My friend and yours from the book by Mary O'Hara.

Iroquois: The first American-bred horse to win the English Derby.

Marengo: The favorite mount of Napoleon, which he rode at Waterloo.

Nelson: General George Washington's white horse seen in all those paintings. He was there at Valley Forge, Yorktown, and Mount Vernon.

Pegasus: The winged horse that carried the thunderbolt of Zeus in Greek mythology. He can be seen today as a constellation.

Sultan: a.k.a. Ivan, the favorite horse of William Cody, a.k.a. Buffalo Bill.

Traveller: General Robert E. Lee's horse, which took him to Appomattox.

You can also get a good discussion of Shakespeare going by quoting the following.

> Imperiously he leaps, he neighs, he bounds.
> His ears up-prick'd; his braided hanging mane
> Upon his compass'd crest now stands on end;
> His nostrils drink the air, and forth again,
> As from a furnace, vapours doth he send;..
> Sometimes he trots, as if he told the steps,
> With gentle majestry and modest pride;
> Anon he rears upright, curves, leaps
> As who should say, "Lo, thus my strength is tried."
>
> (Venus and Adonis)

Words to the Wise

If you are planning on actually faking your way through the act of riding a horse, please, please try to sneak in a few lessons first, whether or not you plan to try riding one in front of others. Breaking your neck impresses no one.

The Human Brain

Being brainy about the brain itself can make you the life of just about any party—provided you're not too obvious in trying to make the point that your brain outranks everyone else's.

Truth be told, most of us have no idea why the brain works or what to do when it doesn't—although that doesn't stop folks from weighing in with opinions about how other people should (or shouldn't) *use* their brains. And for an organ that remains an enigma after centuries of study, brains are certainly the subject of a great deal of attempted manipulation, fast talk, and mass-media hype. The shrewd observation of the Scarecrow from *The Wizard of Oz* remains distressingly relevant: "Some people without brains do an awful lot of talking." It makes you wonder if he watched the most recent batch of televised campaign commercials, doesn't it?

The brain is what makes us who we are...and it's the least understood part of the entire human body. This collection of "little gray cells" (as Agatha Christie's fictional detective Hercule Poirot often refers to his own model) has, over the years, been compared to the abacus, to waterworks, to the steam engine, to simple electric circuits, and to the personal computer. In fact, come to think of it (and isn't thinking what we're discussing?), the brain has always been compared to the highest level of technology humanity has yet managed to establish. Who knows what we'll say it resembles a decade or two from now?

Future comparisons to fusion-driven supercomputers or dilithium crystals notwithstanding, the brain is likely to remain the subject of much guesswork. Scientists are still far from being able to mechanically reproduce, or even define, a human thought. And no one is quite sure why electroshock therapy is able to produce positive results in some mental patients. (The procedure has been compared to slapping the side of a television set that's misbehaving.) We do know a fair amount about the brain's structure and basic growth patterns, though. For a review of some of the most interesting points on the mass of gray stuff that's allowed humanity to journey through space, write masterpieces like *Hamlet* and the Bible, and occasionally file completed tax returns on time, read on.

The Straight Scoop

The human brain is the principal structure of the central nervous system; it is the source of memory, thought, emotions, and bodily control. Composed mainly of neurons and their supporting cells (typically between 100 and 200 billion cells in all), it occupies the skull cavity and weighs roughly three pounds by the time its owner is six years old. The brain is the most protected organ in the human body. Nothing else—not the heart, not the genitals, not the lungs—gets a self-contained bony compartment all to itself. There are actually three layers of protection around the brain: the scalp, the skull, and the cushioning membranes known as the meninges, which also cover the spinal cord.

We know that neurons pass information from one point in the brain to another, but exactly which neurons do what when is a topic of discussion probably best left to the experts. (In other words, don't try to fake your way through that part.) Even though certain regions are strongly associated with certain functions, the brain is constantly reprogramming itself—to use a computer metaphor—to compensate for cell loss, which is ongoing in humans. In some cases, it seems, the brain can even restructure itself to compensate for serious injury or trauma.

Sensory nerve cells feed information to the brain from all parts of the body. The brain analyzes the information and sends out messages or directors through motor nerve cells to muscles and glands, causing them to take the appropriate action. These messages are transmitted in the form of electrical impulses, not unlike electrical circuits in a computer. (There I go again with the computer comparisons.)

Yes, but what *is* the brain? Physically, it's made up of three main parts: the cerebrum (large and located at the top), the cerebellum, and the brain stem. The cerebrum, which is divided into two hemispheres, is active in imagination, memory, and language. The cerebellum processes orders from the cerebrum and monitors bodily movement, issuing automatic commands that make tasks like, say, walking, possible without conscious oversight. The brain stem, which physically links the brain structure to the spinal cord, plays a critical role in coordinating movement involving the left and right sides of the body.

What You Can Say

"There's no demonstrated link between brain mass and intelligence." This goes for both humans and other animals. If you're pressed on the point, mention that elephants have considerably larger brains than either humans or orangutans—but display a much more limited mental capacity. It is true, however, that modern humans have a larger brain, relative to total body size, than our earliest known prehistoric ancestor, Australopithecus.

"A three-year-old child has already lost one-half of the brain cells she possessed at birth." As mentioned above, brain-cell loss is a constant part of human development. Changes in mental capacity associated with aging are apparently triggered by cell loss in specific, critical regions, such as the hippocampus, where neuron loss is associated with reduced memory.

"While we sleep, the brain paralyzes us during the REM (Rapid Eye Movement) phase." That's what keeps people from responding physically during dreams. Sometimes, of course, the temporary deep freeze is imperfect, as when people walk during their sleep, reach out during the night, or start dancing with dreamy vigor to "Losing My Religion"—a song closely associated with another category of REM.

When You Want to Change the Subject...

Casually mention that the presence of the female hormone progesterone, which decreases brain swelling, has been linked to reduced severity of brain damage symptoms in surgical patients— and wonder aloud whether this means that the vast majority of men, are, by definition, functioning at reduced mental capacity (i.e., with swelled heads, and all the attendant trouble *that* can cause), when compared to women. Now you've succeeded in focusing the conversation on the battle of the sexes. The very best of luck to you.

Words to the Wise

Read Dr. Oliver Sacks's endlessly fascinating book, *The Man Who Mistook His Wife for a Hat,* for information on the specifics of a variety of human neurological "misprogrammings."

You should also avoid too many computer-related metaphors in discussions of brain function—at least until computers start programming themselves to compensate for their own deteriorating hardware.

HOW TO IMPRESS ANYBODY ABOUT

The Internet

Hey, some of us are computer people and some of us aren't, right? Here's a quick, and relatively painless, summary of what all the fuss is about. Five minutes here and you can figure out what people are saying, keep up with what your friends are talking about, impress strangers, and save yourself countless hours and untold bucks in online fees.

The Straight Scoop

Think of the Internet (or Net) as a really big CB radio network, not as a piece of computer software. For most users, the Net is simply a means of finding information on, or having conversations about, just about any topic under the sun. Perhaps more importantly, the Internet is a way of making connections based on shared interests—rather than where you are physically. With the Internet, all you have to be near is a computer modem.

Here's how it works. You sign yourself up with an online service company that offers Internet access, like Prodigy or America OnLine or any of hundreds of smaller providers. (People can also access the Internet from an institutional system of some kind.) You get an address that's usually just a name with some computer stuff stuck on the end. It looks like this: yourname@aol.com

If someone knows your address, that person can send messages to you by typing a message and hitting a key to send it off. That's called e-mail. It takes the form of a document you can read on your computer; sometimes, people append sounds and images to their e-mail missives (these are called attachments).

One of the most popular things to do on the Net is to post messages in spots where anyone who feels like it can check them out. These discussion groups are known as Usenet newsgroups. After you've posted a note in one of these places, other people who read it (really, anyone on the face of the earth who has Internet access) can respond in the same place or write you privately. There are also discussion groups that require you to join the group formally, typically by e-mailing a message to a central location, after which you're e-mailed all the relevant correspondence directly. Each of these discussion groups covers a certain common outlook or topic of interest: finding a job, pretending you're a vampire, obsessing about the nefarious intentions of the World Bank, whatever.

There are lots of other things you can do on the Net: pick up software, check reference materials, play games, and so on. But the note-writing thing is one of the two main activities people are likely to bring up when they discuss the Internet. Another, and currently even more popular, part of the Net is known as the World Wide Web (WWW), a picture-intensive network of electronic pages that connect to one another through the use of highlighted keywords. There are Web pages on every conceivable subject, from the soberly academic to the elaborately paranoid to the downright sleazy. Nowadays many Internet providers offer free personalized web pages to new subscribers, which means that there are thousands upon thousands of web pages that detail things like the author's favorite books, résumé, or pets.

What You Can Say

Curious about how to keep the other person talking while you nod knowingly? Ask, "What browser do you use?" Your companion will now hold forth on various types of software. He or she probably won't stop talking for ten minutes or so. If you excuse yourself to get a drink, this may go unnoticed. When you return, you won't have missed anything. If you're asked what browser you use, just say something like this: "They're changing the system around now at work. I never know what they're putting in next."

If pressed on a technical point you don't understand, you can always start complaining about how often your computer system crashes (stops working) during online sessions. Blame everything on the Windows operating system. Your conversational partner will nod sympathetically.

Here are some key terms with which you may need to familiarize yourself:

- A Usenet newsgroup is one of those places to read messages on a certain topic.

- Joining a mailing list means having all the notes of a particular newsgroup forwarded to you automatically.

- A link is a highlighted piece of text that connects one World Wide Web site to another.

- Lurking means reading messages without adding any of your own.

- A modem is the machine that lets one personal computer talk to another via the telephone line. These days, a lot of computers come with modems built in.

- A host computer is one you're visiting with your computer.

- Flaming means sending really rude e-mail or newsgroup correspondence, usually in retaliation for some perceived slight. (Insults take on a whole new meaning online; it's often surprisingly easy to tick someone off.)

- Spamming means sending frivolous, irrelevant, or overtly sales-oriented messages to vast numbers of people who couldn't care less. Modern mail managers make this possible, but they don't make it popular. Spamming makes you about as popular as a chug-a-lug enthusiast at a wine tasting.

- IRC is short for Internet Relay Chat. This refers to a kind of chat group, also called a chatroom. Chat groups converse in real time. In other words, when you send something the person or persons on the other end see it right away, and can answer right away. Online services, and some Web sites, also offer chat rooms. With a few exceptions, chat groups tend to be dim-witted, lewd, or a combination of the two.

When You Want to Change the Subject...

...rejoice, because the Internet covers everything. If you want to start talking about your garden instead, ask your conversational partner if he or she knows of a good Web site on gardening. Write down the address (code that allows you to access) cautiously and carefully, even if you don't plan to use it. Whether or not there is such a site to record, you are now free to start complaining about, or rhapsodizing about, your garden.

Words to the Wise

Some people simply can't stop talking about the Internet. Fortunately, they're usually people you won't miss if you have to excuse yourself to "check on the bean dip."

HOW TO IMPRESS ANYBODY ABOUT

Jazz

Louis Armstrong's famous definition of jazz ("If you have to ask, you'll never know") may still be the last word on the subject. Still, if you're reading this part of the book, it's probably because you have to ask, so let's not let Satchmo's dictum inhibit us. Yes, you can make your way through a discussion of jazz in a matter of minutes. Take a deep breath, get out your black turtleneck, and prepare to become impossibly hip.

The Straight Scoop

Is there a single guiding idea here? Thankfully, yes. Principle Number One: African rhythms—ultimately, inspired by the songs of slaves—mixed with European harmonies to produce...no, not rock and roll (that came later), but jazz. A brief overview of the big movements follows. Your best bet is probably to snag a CD featuring one or more of the artists referenced below. (Start with Louie Armstrong's "Struttin'" with "Some Barbecue Sauce" or "Sweethearts on Parade.")

Ragtime transmogrified into New Orleans, or Dixieland jazz; the form then produced such giants as King Oliver, Jelly Roll Morton, Johnny Dodds, and Louis Armstrong. An exodus of great musicians from New Orleans around 1917 led to various important developments in jazz across America. Here are few easy-to-assimilate ideas that will help you navigate your way impressively through a conversation about the major movements that followed without incident:

Swing: Although the movement had been growing for some decades beforehand under the notable influence of Armstrong, the 1930s marked the zenith of jazz as a popular form of music, and Louis was around to take advantage of the boom. Look for any of Satchmo's stuff, or Benny Goodman's 1938 Carnegie Hall Concert and you'll get a pretty good sense of the new sound that was more than just "all reet." Other not-to-be-missed artists of the period would include Fletch Henderson, Count Basie, and Duke Ellington.

Bebop: And then there was Bird—the incomparable alto sax player Charlie Parker. Along with John "Dizzy" Gillespie and Bud Powell, Parker helped, in the late forties, to create the sound that would inspire Jack Kerouac to go "on the road" and lead a whole generation in search of the "Beat" sound. Look for *The World's Greatest Jazz Concert,* featuring all three aforementioned innovators.

Cool Bop: Miles Davis moves to the forefront in the fifties with his album *Birth of the Cool.* His comrades Dave Brubeck and Jerry Mulligan later took up the charge, and pretty soon jazz musicians everywhere were adding horns and softening their sound. Arrangements became laid back, yet remained multidimensional.

Modal Jazz: "Sheets of sound" was the oft-quoted description of the new direction jazz took following the late fifties. To put it (very) simply, Julian "Cannonball" Adderley, Miles Davis, and John Coltrane began experimenting with "coloring a mode" and layering it with scales. Okay, maybe you have to hear it. All three performers are in evidence on *Kinda Blue.*

Free Jazz: In the sixties, the Beatles weren't the only ones exploring the sounds of India. Eric Dolpy and Ornette Coleman were among those rebelling against the tyranny of the formal chord progression. Listen to Coleman's Double Quartet (which I guess would add up to eight if you're counting along at home).

Afro-Cuban: Chano Pozo had introduced Dizzy Gillespie to the sounds of Cuba. Together with Mike Longo, Stan Kenton, and Tito Puente, Gillespie merged the Latin influence with African rhythms in the 1960s. For a great example of this try *Swing Low Sweet Cadillac.*

Fusion Jazz: Miles Davis had released *Bitches' Brew;* along with musicians like Freddie Hubbard and Herbie Hancock, Davis took jazz to what was perhaps its most experimental stage, incorporating high-tech computer intonation with the classic instrumentation.

What You Can Say

Observations you can deliver more or less word-for-word when the situation warrants:

"Nice cornet solo." And remember, it's cornet (the small trumpet) not coronet (a small crown, and the inspiration for a brand of toilet tissue). Substitute one for the other and you'll make everyone aware that you're not quite the aficionado you claim to be.

"What a shame that we will never hear Louis Armstrong at his peak." (If your companions look at you in shock, calmly explain that Satchmo never recorded any of this music until he was in his thirties, and that his work in the earlier years was, as legend has it, truly peerless.)

If everyone else agrees that the band is a bad one, say wryly, "This group's got all the swing of a dead monkey."

When pressed to defend something you like, quote Duke Ellington: "Didn't Ellington say that if it sounded good, it was good?" Look to the group with wide-eyed innocence.

"Mmmm." When in a club, simply listen with your eyes half closed, nodding occasionally and making nondescript approval noises. At an unexpected moment, you might quietly chuckle to yourself. Applaud after every solo, but clap for some more enthusiastically than others. (When in doubt, follow the crowd on this score.)

When You Want to Change the Subject...

...just stop talking, close your eyes, and move your head in rhythm until the music stops. It will then (probably) be safe for you to speak.

Words to the Wise

If you try to discuss any of the above with actual jazz musicians, you'll come off looking like an amateur. If you're not a musician, then just keep your mouth shut and nod a lot. Offer to buy your companion(s) a drink.

Also bear in mind that jazz fans tend to get nervous whenever any of the stuff they love gets too popular; the appeal is in exclusivity. You might consider saying this: "I've always said...when jazz is embraced by the mainstream is when jazz dies." If anyone challenges you on this, smile knowingly and start talking about something else as though you had no interest in making the other person look foolish.

Newtonian Physics

A famous survey of the one hundred most influential individuals of all time ranked Sir Isaac Newton at number two—right between Muhammad and Jesus Christ. Newton came up with laws that more or less explained the basic structure and operation of the physical universe—or at least did a pretty good job of explaining the universe until that upstart Einstein showed up.

Newton also invented calculus (an honor he is regarded as sharing with Gottfried von Leibniz), thus intimidating untold millions of math-averse high school students, of which I was one. Here's your thumbnail sketch of this extraordinary scientist's most important contributions.

The Straight Scoop

The three laws Newton developed govern the movements of material objects. They may sound fairly straightforward, but they were extraordinary breakthroughs for seventeenth-century science, and must be listed among humanity's most profound scientific achievements.

The first law: Every object tends to move in the same direction it starts in—or, if still, to stay still—unless it's acted upon by an outside force.

The second law: A force applied to an object leads to a rate of change of momentum in direct proportion to the force exerted upon the object, and in the direction of the force. Or, to put the law in its most familiar form, the force to move an object is equivalent to the object's mass times its acceleration (F = MA).

The third law: For every action, there is an equal and opposite reaction.

Coupled with Newton's own earlier work in the area of gravitation, the rules summarized here wiped away centuries of wildly inaccurate conjecture about the nature of the physical world in general, and the solar system in particular. By means of his own newly invented branch of mathematics—calculus—Newton proved that the same principle could be used to explain both falling objects on earth and the movements of celestial bodies. (He explained his rules for the scientific community, however, using familiar geometric tools, rather than the calculus that had served him so well in his private investigations.) Put simply, Newton's new rules worked—consistently and predictably—in ways no other set of rules ever had.

Nowadays, the principles for which Newton is most famous—even that tricky-sounding second law—somehow carry the ring of intuitive truth. Complaining that Newton's laws restate principles that everyone somehow knows, however, is a little like complaining that *Hamlet* is a play crammed with cliches. Newton's work, particularly his three laws of motion, moved human knowledge forward with a dramatic suddenness that has seldom been equalled. They also laid the foundation for modern physics, and are put to continual, reliable use in matters of everyday mechanics three centuries after the death of their originator—even though the clockwork conception of the universe Newton inspired gave way to a more complex model following the revolutionary work of Einstein in the early twentieth century.

In addition to developing the three laws of motion, Newton also discovered and gave form to the law of gravitation and made extraordinary contributions to mathematics, optics, and astronomy. His many and varied contributions to human knowledge are nothing short of mind boggling. (It was Newton, for instance, who demonstrated that white light is made up of numerous colors.) He is widely and just ly regarded as the greatest scientific thinker in human history.

What You Can Say

Between 1664 and 1666, when much of Newton's greatest work was accomplished, he had to work on his own from his home at Wools-thorpe, because Cambridge had been shut down. So much for institutes of higher learning as an aid to research! It was during this period that Newton began his great work on universal gravitation and optics and began to formulate what would become known as the calculus.

"It's probably fair to say that no other scientist, short of Einstein, can claim authorship of a work as influential as the *Principia*." (The full name of Newton's groundbreaking 1687 treatise on terrestrial and celestial mechanics was *Philosophiae Naturalis Principia Mathematica.* That translates as *Mathematical Principles of Natural Philosophy.* Whatever you call it, Newton's treatise was a landmark in modern science and one of the supreme achievements of the human mind.)

"Newtonian physics still gets the job done as a practical matter in everyday situations, of course—it just doesn't serve as the final answer to the fundamental structures of the universe." (The rise of quantum theory and relativity theory—see the separate entries for each—led to extraordinary new insights into the study of matter, energy, and their interrelationship in the physical world.)

When You Want to Change the Subject...

...make reference to the fact that Newton's knighthood was awarded as much for his work as warden of the national mint as for his scientific brilliance. You can then conclude with, "It just goes to show—money talks." Then connect this principle to whatever current example of the same principle comes to mind.

Words to the Wise

No, he had nothing to do during his lifetime with the development of the Fig Newton. Falling apples, maybe. Figs, no.

HOW TO IMPRESS ANYBODY ABOUT

Painting

What is a painting? It's a category of visual art—"a picture or design executed in paints," according to the dictionary—meant to elicit an emotional or intellectual response. This basic idea carries all kinds of interesting implications, some of which can get very complicated indeed. As anyone who's tried faking their way around this topic can attest, entering into a conversation about painting can be a challenging endeavor. It's very easy to fall into a highly competitive game of who can quote which critic about which famous painter.

Rest assured, though, that *how you respond* to a painting by a master like da Vinci, Cézanne, Vermeer, or Pollock is, in the final analysis, more important than what some critic has to say about it. What follows is a basic introduction to some of the major movements in painting. Take it for what it's worth, and then take a look at the work yourself and use your own reactions as the best (and most honest) way of demonstrating your expertise.

The Straight Scoop

There follow descriptions of some major nineteenth- and twentieth-century movements in painting that you may want to consider working into the conversation. *Beware:* Not every great artist or movement is discussed below. And please bear in mind that reading a paragraph about a painting is a poor substitute for examining the work itself.

Abstract expressionism was a movement in American painting during the 1950s that emphasized color, the physical qualities of paint, and the way that paint interacts with the canvas. Many abstract expressionist paintings are so large they could cover an entire wall. *Who was doing it?* Arshile Gorky, Willem de Kooning, Jackson Pollock.

Cubism was a movement in painting (originating in Paris around 1907) that sought to break down objects into the basic shapes of cubes, spheres, cylinders, and cones. The cubists also introduced the dimension of time into painting by presenting various sequential views of objects in the same image. *Who was doing it?* Pablo Picasso, George Braque, Juan Gris, and Fernand Leger.

De stijl ("the style") came out of the Netherlands in 1917, and stressed the purity of line and the use of primary colors. The goal was to use painting to advance toward spiritual purity. *Who was doing it?* Theo van Doesburg, Piet Mondrian, Gerrit Thomas Rietveld, and J. J. P. Oud.

Fauvism was a French movement of the early twentieth century that used bright colors, bold patterns, and brushwork to express the vividness and excitement of nature. *Who was doing it?* George Braque, Raoul Dufy, Georges Roualt, and Maurice de Vlaminck.

Expressionism (a term attributed to a variety of artists at various periods, including a number who worked independent of recognized schools) attempted to convey emotion directly through the use of strong color and simplification of form. Expressionism held that the subjective feelings of one person can be translated onto the canvas. *Who was doing it?* Vincent Van Gogh, Jannes Ensor, and Edward Munch.

Futurism (which arose around 1909 and flourished until the beginning of World War I) fused movement and rhythm to glorify the power, speed, and excitement of the machine age. Futurists broke up realistic forms into multiple images and overlapped fragments of color to show the energy and speed of life. *Who was doing it?* Umberto Boccioni and Antonio Sant'Elia.

Impressionism, one of the most influential movements in painting, is associated with periods in the careers of a number of important artists of the late nineteenth and early twentieth centuries. Impressionism emphasized the use of bright colors and individual brush strokes to convey transitory impressions of light and form. Impressionists often depicted landscapes with a timeless quality, or captured moments of human experience in a luminous way that was sometimes reminiscent of the accidental composition of photography. *Who was doing it?* Camille Pissarro, Édouard Manet, Claude Monet, Pierre-Auguste Renoir, and Mary Stevenson Cassat. ("Post-impressionist" painters strongly influenced by the Impressionist movement include Paul Cézanne, Paul Gaugin, and Vincent Van Gogh.)

Realism, a style of painting in which the rendering of an authentic view of the object or scene is important both visually and emotionally, was inspired by the French Revolution of 1848—and by Europe's move to a more scientific and practical outlook. *Who was doing it?* Gustave Courbet, Jean-Francois Millet, and Honoré Daumier.

Surrealism (popular in the 1920s and onward) often employed extraordinary technical precision to urge viewers to enter the realm of the subconscious mind and ride waves of dreamlike symbolism. The surrealists claim to make forms and images not by reason, but by unthinking impulse and blind feeling. *Who was doing it?* Joan Miro, Salvador Dali, Rene Maquette, Max Ernst, and Giorgio de Chirico.

And now, a word about one of painting's Big Debates—Classic vs. Romantic. When people say that classical works are their cup of tea, they mean that they are drawn to the balance and defined spaces that come together to create a seemingly sublime and harmonious relationship between objects. The object seems not to have been created by a mere human; it appears to carry a perfection that could only be inspired by a greater force. The opposing view is that of the turbulent, mysterious, rebellious romantic who sees the human artist as a poet of sorts—one who, as an individual, feels and sees more than others.

What You Can Say

When looking at an abstract piece you like: "What impresses me is the artist's ability to reveal an underlying clarity and logic toward the subject."

When looking at a very small piece you like: "It's incredible—a whole world right here, in harmony."

When looking at a very big piece: "I'd like to see the living room that one came out of."

When looking at a religious subject you like, consider mentioning something about the Renaissance view of the fundamental humanity of religion—as opposed to the more rigid forms of the Middle Ages or even idealized images of the gods belonging to ancient cultures.

When looking at a somber piece you like: "Ahh, the loneliness . . ."

When looking at food in a painting you like: "It has a very erotic quality, don't you think?" Feign a shocked attitude, then smile mischievously.

When looking at a piece that's provocative or downright disgusting: "Well, you have to admire an artist who can involve you whether you want to be involved or not."

When You Want to Change the Subject...

It only works once, but it's quite reliable: Art always makes me famished. "Did you know they have a very good restaurant [downstairs/upstairs/next door/wherever]? Shall we?" Another good strategy is to discuss the current events taking place during the artist's lifetime, and in that way move into a discussion of (a familiar stretch of) history. See the dates connected with each of the major schools discussed above.

Words to the Wise

Make the right impression while at the museum. Dress with respect, as though you were going to religious services. (In many ways, you are.) When you enter the museum, take a deep breath, as if you were taking in the very atmosphere, thick as it is with art. Chat in hushed tones, just above a whisper. When entering a new room, walk first to the smallest painting or sculpture. Save the biggest stuff for last. Regardless of its size, walk up close to the piece and bend forward to inspect it closely. Then back away about three steps and smile to yourself. For the big stuff, take a look from a distance (like across the room), then smile.

Feel free to read everything posted on the walls, but remember—the more surreptitious you are about this, the better. You'd be surprised at the depth of information you can get right there on the wall. When leaving the museum take another deep breath, as if your very soul had been renewed.

HOW TO IMPRESS ANYBODY ABOUT

Palmistry

Want to be the guaranteed hit of any party? Take a moment or two to familiarize yourself with a few of the principles of palmistry.

There are two great things about conducting a palm reading session. First and foremost, you get to hold hands with members of the opposite sex, which can be pretty cool, and second, whether or not you have any skill as a palm reader, you get to tell people things you already know to be true about them and watch as they stare back at you in stunned amazement. No, I'm not advocating that you start auditioning for a spot at the local county fair—unless you feel like it, of course.

Basically, I'm going to offer you some information on ways you can impress others with their own hands. In "The Straight Scoop," below, I'll give the a condensed summary of the principles used by palm readers to develop theories. This information is (many of us believe) on the level when used by someone with the gift. In "What to Say," which follows, I'll show you how to finagle a truth that you both may want to hear. Just promise me that you will use these powers only for good.

The Straight Scoop

When palm readers do their thing, they're looking at a lot more than the lines in the palm. The shape of the palm and the fingers can also tell volumes. The way the person places a hand in yours; the texture of the skin; even the placement of scratches, callouses, and condition of the nails can say a lot.

The shape of the hand is the foundation of your reading. Everyone jumps to the lines, especially the heart- and life-line, to learn what they want to know. But these can vary because of the shape of the hand. Also important: the position of the hand. What gestures does the person make while you do your reading? In other words, watch the body language while you talk to your subject. Should a palm turn to a clenched fist, I'd stop, say everything looks swell, and head for the onion dip.

To start, ask the person to place both hands in your open hands. Softly, in a caring fashion, touch the hands gently, turning them over to examine both sides. Note the temperature and the texture of the hands. Do this by looking at the hands first, and then at the person. You're looking for any sense of tension or apprehension. Is the person excited, laughing, enthusiastic, tense?

Explain that it would be a bit of an oversimplification to pretend that the hands tell you what the person is like, or that the lines and marks thereon tell the future, but that you're going to assume that this is possible and do a reading anyway. (After all, people will be impressed by what you tell them they know to be true. This will lend credence to what you say later.)

Does the person have small hands? If so, she may be a happy person ready for whatever fun might come her way. She's also great to have as a friend when the chips are down. This person understands others and is a good listener. She will often know how to make a person feel comfortable, even someone whom she doesn't know well. She may be easily bored, and on the lookout for the next adventure.

Does the person have large hands? This is a person who finds pleasure in the details. This person is frustrated by projects that he cannot complete to perfection. Among his assets are his powers of concentration. He is most comfortable in surroundings that he knows well. People with large hands are thought by palmistry pros to be dependable and are deeply caring about the causes that concern them.

Does the person have square palms? This is easy to determine; look at the bottom corners of the palm. Square palms mean that this person is focused on the bottom line. She wants results and she wants them now. She's probably respected for her ability to get the most for her money and her time.

Does the person have round palms? Round-palmed people are thought to be charmers. They are warm and well liked. They are optimistic and enjoy life. They're probably the life of whatever party they attend. They may be social butterflies—people who know exactly where the action is and how to get there.

Does the person have spatulate palms? (Spatulate is a fancy word that means "broad and flat, like a spatula.") This person is said to long for adventure. She's likely to be a risktaker, a lone wolf. She often spends her time looking for the next mountain to climb or the next ocean to cross. She may settle down for a time but she's likely, in the end, to wander again, seeking out the next new place. She feels things deeply and is protective of other people's emotions.

Does the person have thick hands? These people are, palmists believe, the doers, the people who know how to get the job done and do it. The person with thick hands will take on almost any project and enjoy every minute of doing it. Sometimes he finds himself overextended, but he will still find a way to succeed at the task. He's likely to become a person of high profile.

Does the person have thin hands? This is the sensitive dreamer. Her imagination is the key to her success. Though she may feel things more deeply than others, she is also most likely to be the person to find solutions to problems. This person needs a peaceful and tranquil environment in which to blossom. She may be a fantastic caregiver who is highly attuned to the feelings of others.

Does the person have short palms? In other words, is the palm exactly as wide as it is tall? This type of palm is also called a square palm. People with square palms, besides being result-oriented, are thought to be emotionally strong individuals. They take what comes in stride and they welcome any and every challenge. These natural-born leaders are great in a crisis. They make decisions quickly. They look forward to what the day brings them.

Does the person have long palms? Longer than it is wide, this hand shows a person who reveres the past, and balks at change. This person is happiest when surrounded by things he loves and by objects that have a history. "Days of yore" are almost always remembered fondly. This person always seems to be the one to remember birthdays and anniversaries. Long palms are the mark of good friends—and, quite often, friends for life.

Does the person have long fingers? This is an analytical person. This person may have a terrific memory. She will probably know a great deal about the subjects that interest her— and many subjects do. She is patient and loyal, and values friendship highly.

Does the person have short fingers? Wow! Watch out for this firecracker. Quick to make decisions and friends, this person will get to the heart of the matter. His instincts for reading situations and people can be highly accurate. However, when he's wrong, he often pays a large emotional price.

Does the person have long thumbs? If so, he may be a born leader, someone who will carry through to the end.

Does the person have short thumbs? She may be a follower, a diplomat; someone who prefers peace to action.

Does the person have pink palms? He's likely to be a high-energy person. (A pale palm is taken as a sign that the owner may be in need of some time out, or may have some problems with low energy levels.)

What does the person's skin feel like? Thin skin is said to reflect the outlook of a thinker and a feeler, someone who seeks harmony and loves luxury. Coarse skin may belong to someone who reacts well to stress, who prefers to take individual action, who dislikes leaving important matters to others. Skin in the middle may mean you're dealing with a flexible person, someone who can get things done—but not at the expense of another's happiness.

Are the person's hands firm or soft? A firm hand may indicate someone who's a natural leader, and who can be stubborn on subjects about which he feels strongly. A soft pair of hands, on the other hand, may mean the person is kind and thoughtful, but may have a tendency to give in to others too often or too easily.

What do the nails look like? Large? You may be dealing with a person of great energy, someone who relaxes by doing, who's fascinated by doing detail work. *Small?* You may well have hooked up with a "people person," someone who enjoys interacting with people and enjoys helping others—but you may run out of energy from time to time, and you should focus on pacing yourself. *Round nails* are said to belong to people who are intuitive and helpful, those who are known for being fairminded and for enjoying current trends and an active social life. *Square nails,* on the other hand, are said to belong to the perfectionist, the person who believes herself to be in the right—and who expects a lot from herself and the people around her. (Square-nailed people are also said to enjoy technical pursuits; they may have a strong need to feel useful.) How about *spatulate nails?* (Broad and flat, remember?) These folks are adventurers and groundbreakers who may be both restless and curious; they're said to be enthusiastic and willing to try anything at least once. Don't try to pin them down.

Of mounts, lines, and all that. (Note: From here on out, you're looking at the hand the person uses *least* during the course of the day.) There are pads at the base of each finger and around the outside edge of the hand. Each of these has a name and a meaning attributed to that area. Any marks or lines appearing in that area have a meaning as well. Each finger has a name given to it and prescribes a direction or attribute your life may take. The index finger is *Jupiter/ The Leader.* The middle finger is *Saturn/The Thinker.* The ring finger is *Apollo/The Creator,* and the little finger is *Mercury/The Genius.* The thumb has no parallel name and is read by the pattern of its finger print. The pad under each finger is called a mount, and is named in reference to its corresponding finger. (For example: "the mount of Jupiter.") The large mount under the thumb is called the *Mount of Venus/The Lover.* The mount directly opposite this, on the edge of the palm, is the *Mount of Luna/The Dreamer.* Above this mount and directly under the mount of Mercury is the small *Mount of Upper Mars/The Fighter.* Across from this in between the Mount of Venus and the Mount of Jupiter is the *Mount of Lower Mars/The Fighter.*

The Heart Line is the line that describes all of your emotions. It is located horizontally across your hand, directly under the mounds of each finger. It is the topmost long horizontal line, running from your pinkie finger to just under your first finger (or beyond). *The Head Line* shows the way your mind works. It can be found horizontally just below the heart line. It runs usually from just under the index finger to just past the ring finger. *The Life Line* is often thought of as the line that will tell you how long you will live; in truth, it's supposed to tell you what will cross your path as you live it. It can be found curving along the Mount of Venus near the thumb.

Interpreting the lines means more than just looking at the obvious major creases. There are also small lines and shapes that can have great meaning depending on which mount they appear on. *Vertical lines* increase the positive meaning of the mount. *Horizontal lines* show an obstacle to achieving the talents or strengths of the mount. *Slanting lines* highlight the influences of other people on this mount. *Single bar lines* represent challenges that are now emerging. A *grille* means confusion is indicated in the area in question. *Crosses* reflect a special ability concerning the mount that may be unfulfilled as of yet. *Squares* mean you should protect this area; there is danger toward it. *Triangles* represent a show of talent. *Circles* are rare; they mean that the unexpected will occur in the area in question. *Stars* are pretty rare too; they represent success and recognition to be achieved.

What's it all add up to? Well, if the person whose hand you're examining has vertical lines in the Mount of Venus, then you may conclude that she's well loved, but if there is a square in the same region, there may be a love that will be lost if she does not stay on her guard. A star on the Mount of Jupiter may mean a big success on the job, or in one of many hidden talent areas.

Expect your subject to pose questions. The most often asked questions are those about love and success; by following the above markings you should be able take a stab at some interpretations of each of the regions of the hand. As with anything else, the more you practice, the better you will get.

You will probably be surprised by how great the differences can be from one person's hand to another. Also, an individual's hands will change dramatically within a very short time. A threat that was apparent one month will be gone the next. A romance may just as easily appear within the same time frame.

What You Can Say

Now for the fun part—faking your way through a palm reading. From here on out, I'm going to assume that you're not all *that* interested in actually interpreting the various regions of the hand, as outlined above. Using the terms you have learned above and what you know about the person already, you can perform quite a successful reading by making massive, but strangely persuasive, generalizations about the subject's life.

Notice the feel of the person's hand in yours. If the person's tense, pat his or her hand. Look at the hand carefully and say, "You need to relax more, you're not being good enough to yourself." (No one imagines that he's good enough to himself. Everybody needs a rest. If the subject feels tense, he probably is. If he says he's just been on vacation, come back with... "Then you need a vacation from your vacation."" Again, this is always true to some extent. Ask anyone who's come back from a trip to Disney World with three kids.)

If the hand is relaxed and opened to you, the person probably is too. Say: You're confident and a born adventurer." If the person offered her hand to you without prompting, say... "You're a born leader." (If the person shows no fear or hesitation, then confidence is obvious. If the person takes the initiative by thrusting hands into yours, then you can safely comment on assertiveness or leadership qualities.)

Look for paper cuts or pen marks. Find any? Or does the person's attire, bearing, or conversation about work lead you to believe you're dealing with someone who works in an office? You're in luck. Say: "I see you in front of a desk; there's an endless stream of work for you to complete during the course of the day." When your subject nods in agreement, say: "You must find joy in the doing or look for work elsewhere. If you do that, you'll be happier." (Talk about your blinding flash of the obvious.)

Let's assume that you know the person has his own business, or are able to deduce as much. Say: "You worry too much; you must remember why it is that you do what you do. I see that you are a very caring person, and that what you want most is a happy, secure life. Basically, you want to be able to provide for those you love." (You're taking a little bit of a risk here, but not much. Anybody brave enough to have his own business will be worried from time to time. If you can spot a workaholic and a wedding ring, you can make the logical inference that the person is motivated by a concern to improve his family's lot in life.)

No matter who's sitting across the table, say: "I see a man in your future" if you're talking to a woman, and "I see a woman in your future" if you're talking to a man. (Come on; everybody has someone from the opposite sex come into his or her life. What they make of that event, of course, is their business.)

Say: "It's time for you to let go of a certain disappointment that you suffered as a child." Then get ready for the waterworks—your subject may go into Instant Self-Guided Therapy Mode. (Who doesn't have a closet full of childhood disappointments?)

Reading a boss's palm? Go for the funny stuff: "You are a powerful person who is both respected and feared; at the same time you're also remarkably attractive to others. People enjoy being around you." (Okay, okay; this is an unusually good opportunity to do some brown-nosing. Make the most of it, but at the same time keep your sense of humor—make what you're doing obvious and just a little bit broad.) Do not offer insights on the physical attractiveness of a superior of the opposite sex unless you've got great interpersonal skills that will make it clear that you're not launching a come-on.

When reading the palm of someone who reports to you, you might say: "You love your boss, and you're brave, trustworthy, and hardworking." You might also say: If the person *doesn't* report to you, and you know she's fairly well down in the pecking order, consider this: "Your work is not appreciated enough." (Not exactly a high-risk shot. Everyone feels underappreciated.)

You can tell *almost* everyone whose palm you read that you see a trip with many unpredictable events. (That ninety-year old grandmother who's confined to a wheelchair may be an exception.) Tell half that the journey may be shorter than they expect, and the other half that it may be longer. (Could be the grocery store; could be Spain. How should you know? You're not psychic.)

When You Want to Change the Subject...

Say: "You have an unusually complex character; I'm having some difficulty getting any more from the reading. There's something unfinished in your life, some balance you need to restore. Once you've attended to whatever unfinished business awaits you, we may be able to learn more together."

Words to the Wise

Let people know that they are the real masters of their future; wonder aloud what role fate plays in our lives. For your own part, accept that what palm reading really does is make the subject feel good about himself—and make you seem a little more mysterious than you are.

HOW TO IMPRESS ANYBODY ABOUT
Philosophy

One woman's definition of philosophy: Reason plus logic plus mathematics plus physics plus faith; shake well in a large glass, and serve with a good-sized grain of salt.

The dictionary definition of philosophy is a little more enlightening (but not much): "The search, by logical reasoning, for understanding of the basic truths and principles of the universe, and of human perception and understanding of these."

Nothing like setting the bar high, I always say. Once you've read this part of the book, you'll have a thorough understanding of the basic truths and principles of the universe, and of your own perception and understanding of these. That's my promise to you, the reader. But don't hold me to it.

The Straight Scoop

Socrates, the first established teacher of philosophical thought, never wrote down any of his ideas—but Plato, one of his biggest fans, did. Back then it was quite the thing for a well-born young man to follow an old teacher around while he asked you mindblowing questions designed to break down the walls of what you had previously assumed to be reality. Then, he'd pose a series of questions and stories designed to bring you back to a clearer understanding of what *was* real and what wasn't.

By doing this sort of thing, Socrates publicized his ideas, notably his observations that the essences of things are more real than the aspects that are experienced by outsiders, and that all virtues lead toward the good—the knowledge of one's true nature and purpose in life. Socrates also made waves. Athenian authorities convicted him on obscure charges of impiety and corrupting the morals of youth. Socrates's dutiful but unrepentant death—he drank a dose of hemlock after refusing to concede anything to his accusers—is one of history's great examples of holding to principles, even at the cost of one's own life.

Martyrs, the Athenian powers soon learned, can be more difficult than living people. Soon Socrates's ideas were more influential than ever. Plato started his own school, the Academy, and took up where Socrates left off, eventually coming up with many powerful notions of his own, including his theory that ideal forms exist outside of the material world. His most influential works are *The Symposium*, which focuses on the true nature of love, and *The Republic,* a massively influential series of observations on good government that often reflects Plato's distrust of democracy. (That distrust is not at all surprising, considering the anti-elitist justifications offered for Socrates's public humiliation and death.) Much of what we know about Socrates comes to us through Plato's writings. Both men are associated with the practice of constantly questioning assumptions in a quest for higher truth.

Enter Plato's student Aristotle, who, after studying at the Academy, started his own school, the Lyceum. Like Plato, Aristotle emerged as one of the greatest minds of the ancient world; he's notable primarily for his insistence on emphasizing empirical fact and logical reasoning in both science and philosophy, and for disagreeing with Plato on the subject of ideal forms. (Aristotle believed that form and matter are united.) Aristotle served as the tutor of the conqueror Alexander the Great, although the degree to which the famous instructor's ideas rubbed off on his student is certainly open to debate.

Greece declined, Rome rose, and philosophy and the search for peace of mind followed. Soon the big names in philosophy included that of Lucretius, who argued that fear in the face of death is unnecessary, since the soul is composed of atoms and natural laws govern all phenomena, including the creation of the universe. Later, a Roman emperor, Marcus Aurelius, offered a starkly different perspective based on concepts of duty, piety, reason, and an understanding of the relationship between God and man as tools for overcoming life's many adversities. Lucretius's body of work is categorized as epicurean, after Epicurus, whose work Lucretius studied. Marcus Aurelius's diaries are considered classics of the Stoic school.

Early modern philosophy can be said to start with René Descartes, who put forth his big idea quite succinctly: "Cogito ergo sum." (" I think, therefore I am.") By this he meant, that in a world of complete uncertainty, humans can be certain of their own existence by means of their own status as thinking entities. Descartes also asked important questions about the nature of knowledge and perception, and argued for a "dualism" between mind and body that evoked both the ideas of Plato and certain principles of Christian theological thought.

The big questions, for Descartes and many of those who followed him, were these: Can people prove with total certainty that they have knowledge of events in the external world? And if so, what kind of knowledge is that? Baruch Spinoza continued Descartes's notion that reasoning, on its own, can result in absolute knowledge; this point of view is known as Rationalism. The Empiricists (among them John Locke and George Berkeley) felt otherwise, and argued that knowledge is a matter of experience, rather than reason. Building a bridge between the two schools of thought was Immanuel Kant, who acknowledged the importance of utilizing both points of view, and who strove to show that the human mind, rather than being an impartial receptor, is an active participating factor in human experience.

A more pragmatically oriented series of philosophical questions was put forward by those writing about political and economic philosophy. Important writers in this area include Niccolo Machiavelli, Thomas Hobbes, Jean-Jacques Rousseau, and John Stuart Mill.

Other important schools of philosophical thought included Idealism (the notion, propounded by G. W. F. Hegel and disputed by

Schopenhauer, that the external world, rather than being "real," is based in the human mind) and Existentialism (a school, associated with Soren Kirkegaard, Friedrich Nietzsche, and Jean-Paul Sartre, that focuses intently on matters of being as a backdrop for important questions on choice, faith, free will, and existence itself).

In recent years, important philosophical movements have included that of the Pragmatists (one of whom was William James), who argued that the most useful, relevant, or instructive theories, rather than the most elegantly reasoned ones, are worthiest of attention; the Logical Positivists (among them Bertrand Russell), who dismissed larger questions of meaning and truth that were divorced from direct experience; and those who pursued the Deconstruction approach (such as Jacques Derrida), who search out the essence of meaning by disassembling language and its assumptions, and analyzing the connective units of speech or writing.

What You Can Say

Philosophy is one of those subjects where caution is probably your best bet; the less you say, the smarter you're going to sound. A basic knowledge of the major trends (see above), a few phrases and the right attitude will take you far. After all, remember that most of these guys are talking about abstract issues to which there are no concrete answers. When talking philosophy, asking the right questions will have you looking more in the know than answering any. So if you're asked a question, answer it with a question.

Here are three possible ways to go:

"I guess it all comes back to the allegory of the cave, doesn't it?" (The famous story, which appears in Plato's *Republic,* argues that a human being who has not been properly instructed is like someone chained in a cave, who sees only shadows moving on a wall and assumes them to be the objects themselves. Plato argued that it was possible for such a person to move closer to the light of the highest good by means of disciplined intellectual development that emphasizes the challenging of earlier assumptions.)

"Does Descartes's insistence on the separation of mind and matter still get people's blood boiling?" (Descartes, ever the mathematician, wanted proofs for everything, but ignited a series of long-running battles with his declarations that mind and body were utterly separate.)

"Why should Kierkegaard be credited with founding a school of philosophy? Isn't existentialism—whether it takes place in the nineteenth century or the twentieth—simply a series of depressing rants?" (Kierkegaard's fixation on religion and suffering, and the later ideas extracted from it, have led more than one commentator to dismiss existentialism as a series of brilliantly phrased fits of depression, rather than a system of philosophy meant to illuminate fundamental truths.)

When You Want to Change the Subject...

... quote Nietzsche's summation of Socrates ("the patron saint of moral twaddle") and point out that hard-and-fast standards that everyone can agree on have proved very hard to come by in philosophy. Wonder aloud whether the same could be said of (insert topic of your choice here).

Words to the Wise

Don't actually try to read Kant's *Critique of Pure Reason*. You may permanently damage your own internal machinery.

HOW TO IMPRESS ANYBODY ABOUT

Photography

These days, it's hard to find somebody who doesn't own some sort of a camera. From the point-and-shoot disposables found in drugstores to the intimidating state-of-the-art equipment favored by pros, cameras are just about everywhere and are used, at one time or another, by just about everybody. Here are some hints on how to come off looking, well, focused during your discussions of photography.

The Straight Scoop

The way you sound in a conversation about photography will probably depend on the accuracy of your own assessment of whether or not you're talking to another novice or a real shutterbug.

Setting aside photojournalists, photography fans can be divided into two distinct types: Those who love the equipment and those who love the art form. My advice on dealing with the technophile who owns all the latest equipment is simple: Smile and nod pleasantly. When he or she asks what you shoot just say you're old fashioned; you use "Dad's old Leica." If pressed for specifics, get a little misty-eyed about your personal philosophy of photography, and say that you never really bother with such details: "I'm afraid I take a pragmatic approach—I mean, if Edward Weston can use a light bulb for an enlarger, who needs to get worked up about brand names? I always say it's the end product that matters." Smile knowingly and start looking for the hors d'oeuvres.

What You Can Say

"The history of photography? Easy!" To make your way through a conversation about photography with a beginner, it helps to know something about the origins of the camera itself.

"Well, I suppose that, ultimately, photography has to be traced back to the first use of the camera obscura, doesn't it?" Camera obscura means dark room, but this isn't the type of darkroom contemporary photographers use to develop pictures. This was a dark box—often big enough to stand in—that featured a small hole on one side. Light entered through a minute hole and formed, on the opposite wall, an inverted image of what lay outside. The images could be traced. By the eighteenth century, the room had become a portable (and often essential) tool for artists who wanted to capture a sense of realism without all the work. The camera obscura had been discussed long before Leonardo da Vinci sketched out a design of one. Whoever invented it, the camera obscura was the start of something big.

You can impress by saying, "The French took the world's first photograph—and they've been insufferable about it ever since." In 1826, Joseph Nicéphore Niepce created that first photograph: a nice, if blurry, shot of his front yard. And to think it only took him a whole day to expose the picture onto asphalt! However, it was another Frenchman, Louis Daguerre, who won worldwide fame for advancing the process of permanently capturing an image. His technique became known as the daguerreotype (so much for humility). Before long, lots of people wanted their likenesses preserved in this way. However, the daguerreotype was not reproducible, and it required the use of chemicals that left lots of people loopy on the toxic fumes they were breathing in their unventilated darkrooms.

Photographs became more practical once the images could be rendered onto paper. This accomplishment came about thanks to William Henry Fox Talbot, one of the major figures in the development of photographic processes. Initially, the image on Talbot's calotypes, as he called them, came out as negative versions of the scene captured, but eventually Talbot figured out how turn his negative into a positive.

If you want, you can talk about the emerging role photography played as an artist's tool and as an aid to those who sought to record history:

"The beginning of the Civil War" you can say knowledgeably, "brought about the rise of photojournalism, thanks to men like Matthew Brady." Brady captured images of people, celebrations, and battlefields, for posterity ... even if it did mean moving around a few bodies here and there to set up the "right" shot. Later photographers would follow suit using their (quite cumbersome) cameras to bring all manner of images—disasters, noteworthy individuals, and so on—into the home of the average citizen.

Continue by talking about how photography spread to the world of the nonexpert.

You can say, "Eastman was the great democratizer of the form." Everyday folks gained access to the magic of photography thanks to the efforts of George Eastman. For a fee of twenty-five dollars, Eastman provided a box camera, which someone with virtually no training could use to take pictures. The user would then return the camera to the company to develop, and, wonder of wonders, the pictures would come back in a few weeks by mail. For the first time, anybody could be a photographer, even someone who knew nothing about the technical processes that made it possible! This successful marketing campaign marked the beginning of the period of photography of the people, by the people, and for the people—and of countless amateur photographic beheadings, in which the region above the shoulders never quite makes it into the frame.

Now, of course, we have any number of choices when it comes to cameras and developing our pictures—including the rebirth of the shoot-it-and-turn-it-in camera. (Today's variety, of course, is disposable, and gets dropped off at the supermarket or drugstore.)

Sometimes, you have to be ready to drop some names, or at least respond intelligently to those dropped by the other person. When trying to hold your own with an expert, you should probably be aware of some of the bigger players in the history of photography and photojournalism.

In addition to those already mentioned, major figures in the history of photography include:

Alfred Stieglitz: The father of photography as art. (Interesting side note: Stieglitz was married, for a time, to the artist Georgia O'Keeffe.)

Ansel Adams: Chronicler of a vast world—perhaps the most influential outdoor photographer in history.

Edward Steichen: The supreme architectural photographer; Steichen offered masterful images of bridges and skyscrapers.

Henri Cartier-Bresson: Intimacy among the crowds. Known for capturing the moment.

Margaret Bourke-White: A giant in the history of photojournalism, she went where no woman had gone before, and captured hundreds of historic images of down-on-their-luck farmers, flyboys, concentration camp victims, and, just for good measure, Mahatma Gandhi.

Dorothea Lange: She brought a unique warmth and sensitivity to her images of Dust Bowl farmers and other casualties of the Depression, pictures that made the human costs of the period a reality for millions of Americans.

Edward Weston: Can a rotting green pepper be sexy? Weston had everyone taking cold showers and not knowing exactly why.

George Eastman: Founder of Kodak (a word he made up); those in the know often refer to him as, "Our great yellow father."

Richard Avedon: Masterful fashion and portrait photographer, known for the occasional strange juxtaposition. It's not just a dress, it's a dress with two elephants!

Diane Arbus: A nervous, edgy, alienated photographer for a nervous, edgy, alienated time. Her images of transvestites, dwarves, and nudists reflected her own fearlessness and boundless energy. These forces were not, unfortunately, enough to keep her from committing suicide at an early age.

Annie Leibowitz: Renowned for her ability to capture personality, sometimes by getting very famous people to do strange and exotic things, like take their clothes off (John Lennon) or paint their faces blue (the Blues Brothers).

Helmut Newton: Purveyor of a new, and very glamorous, over-the-top style that ripples with, um, sex.

Robert Mapplethorpe: The bad boy of photography was a superb technician whose elegant (and yes, frequently overt) homoeroticism has led to controversy. Don't let the whips distract you so much that you miss the flowers.

When You Want to Change the Subject...

When you've run out of fascinating facts, the best idea is to stun your listener into silence with a profound observation like this one: "These days photographs are so easy to manipulate digitally that the core idea behind the form—that photography is truth—is often lost in the shuffle. I'm not sure if that is a blessing or a curse."

If that doesn't buy you a few seconds of silence, nothing will. While your listener is mulling over the question, you may be able to slip quietly into a darkened room of your own.

Words to the Wise

Conversational improvisation skills will only take you so far. It probably wouldn't hurt to hit the library and take a brief look at some of the images these folks churned out.

Psychology

Anybody who's anybody has either been in therapy or knows somebody who should be. That means being able to talk about psychology intelligently is probably a good idea. Below, you'll find some ideas that should make it relatively easy to impress new acquaintances.

The Straight Scoop

Any discussion of psychology can be enriched by a basic understanding of the work of the two giants in the field. The first of these giants was...

Sigmund Freud. Say what you will about Freud's theories today, his extraordinary influence on questions of human development and identity is indisputable. Freud is the founder of psychoanalysis; he developed the theory of the Oedipus complex for males and the Electra complex for females. The idea here is that there is an unconscious desire on the part of a child to have sex with the parent of the opposite gender.

Freud not only defined the subconscious but divided it into three parts; the Id, the Ego, and the Superego. He then defined the three stages of human development: the Oral, the Anal, and the Genital stage. When each of these stages is reached in the right order and at about the right time, all is well. If, however, you stop at one stage or skip one, you've got trouble—at least according to Freud. The validity of these stages has been vigorously discussed since they were first hypothesized—especially the third stage—when boys and girls supposedly stop focusing on hunger and control of their bowels, and start fixating on what's between their legs. It's at this stage, Freudians argue, we start desiring sexual intercourse with the parent of the opposite sex. The theory was controversial at the time, and remains so today.

The Id, Ego, and Superego structure has its detractors, too, but it's just as fascinating. According to Freud, we are born with the Id. It is an instinctive part of our subconscious; it reflects basic aggression and sexual impulses. The Ego is our own personal safety valve; it slows us down and attempts to control these Id-based urges. And the Superego is the "parental voice" of our subconscious, which tries to hold us to the social standards of the world in which we live.

Freud's work was hugely influential, as was that of the second giant in the field of psychology ...

Carl Gustav Jung. Jung was Freud's student; he broke with the master and proceeded to put forth his own ideas concerning the subconscious. Jung, who was less interested in exploring the consequences of repression than Freud was, came up with the idea of the complex, a grouping of ideas and images that may appear unrelated but are charged with meanings and emotions deriving from the subconscious. Jung also divided people into two categories—introverts and extroverts—and expounded a theory of a feminine principle within men (the *anima*) and a masculine principle within women (the *animus*). Perhaps most influentially, Jung held that cultures and humanity at large share a common pool of images, patterns, and personages—a collective unconscious expressed through such channels as dreams and myths—that he called Archetypes.

There have been many, many developments in the study of mental processes in the years since these two towering figures did their extraordinary work, but a basic understanding of the main ideas associated with Freud and Jung should be enough to get you started. (And, for the record: Psychiatrists are—in the U.S.—medical doctors who study mental disorders and maladjustments and propose treatments for these; psychologists are those who study mental processes, both healthy and unhealthy. Some U. S. psychologists also offer therapy, but they're not M.D.s.)

What You Can Say

"Freud's theory of penis envy could well be just another example of the sexism of his era." (According to his detractors, the penis envy Freud expounded reveals his own prejudices. Apparently, they argue, the doctor was of the opinion that girls wanted a penis, because—well, because who doesn't?)

"Sometimes, Freud makes me wonder who's really fixated on the genitals—his patients, or Freud himself." (In contrast, you might point out that Jung placed much less emphasis on the question of how one felt about one's private parts.)

"Jung was interested in exploring the expression of thoughts and ideas—why they happen and how they manifest themselves." (He also argued that the collective unconscious was composed of common symbols, or archetypes.)

"Jung was the first psychologist to explore the idea of 'synchronicity.'" (Synchronicity is the way seemingly unrelated events can come together to yield surprisingly on-target results in both analysis and general decision-making.)

"Freud and Jung both felt that dreams often lead the way to the truth behind our conscious awareness." (Both argued that there is a subconscious self at work in everyday human life and that not everything is what it appears to be on the surface.)

When You Want to Change the Subject...

When the opportunity presents itself, wonder aloud what the cigar-chomping Freud would make of the growing disapproval of tobacco, once a universal addiction among most adults, and now regarded with almost universal abhorrence as being among the most distasteful of oral fixations. You might mention that Freud himself was a cigar smoker and died, painfully, of cancer.

Words to the Wise

Don't start talking about pens, sausages, levers, trains, keys, thumb-tacks, bananas, paintbrushes, screwdrivers, flower stems, or anything else vaguely phallic with a really strict Freudian. Unless you've got a lot of time on your hands.

HOW TO IMPRESS ANYBODY ABOUT

Quantum Theory

Our ideas about energy and motion were changed forever by the formulation of quantum theory by Max Planck in 1900 and the Uncertainty Principle in 1927 by Werner Heisenberg. Herewith is a layman's introduction to quantum mechanics, which, together with the Theory of Relativity (*see separate entry:* "Einstein's Theory of Relativity"), forms the basis of modern theoretical physics. Get all this straight and you'll even impress yourself!

The Straight Scoop

What's the deal with the uncertainty in the uncertainty principle? After all, isn't science a matter of fixed results, predictable outcomes, and stable, all-controlling laws—like the ones Newton put forth? (*See separate entry:* "Newtonian Physics.") Well, in the world of quantum mechanics, maybe not.

Quantum theory holds that, at the atomic and subatomic level, energy is not a fixed entity—that it does not possess a constant range of values, but is, on the contrary, radiated and absorbed in a disoriented (and, perhaps, disorienting) way. As the theory has it, no one can state with perfect accuracy two properties of an indivisible quantum object—for instance, both the position and the concurrent momentum of a particle. (The more accurate your measurement of one property is, the less accurate your measurement of the other property becomes. For example, if the momentum of a particle is measured with complete accuracy, its exact position can't be found because it moved while you were busy figuring out how fast it was going.) These effects, according to quantum theory, can be predicted and expressed only in the language of probability—the chance, not the certainty, that a certain outcome will take place.

Still with me? Things gets stranger. Quantum theorists observed that light, which is generally seen as a wave, could, in some ways, be perceived as being made up of individual particles, known as photons. By the same token, quantum theory holds that atomic particles (electrons, for instance) can be said to have wavelike characteristics.

What it all boils down to is that, at the level of the atom and below, energy itself does not vary in a continuous, predictable way, as might be expected on the large-scale environment most of us are familiar with. That's the environment that Newtonian physics does such a superb job of predicting. When the discussion turns to atoms, nuclei, and elementary particles, however, things get a lot more... uncertain. The basis of uncertainty principle, as we've seen, is that you cannot measure *both* the velocity and position of a particle.

What You Can Say

"Basically, energy has a way of acting as though it's a wave at some times, and as though it consists of particles at other times." (This is probably your best shot at a single-sentence summary of quantum theory.)

Or try this: "Unlike Newton's one-man revolution in physics, the twentieth century development of quantum theory was the work of many great scientists. Among them, Planck, Heisenberg, Albert Einstein, and Niels Bohr."

Or this: "Just as the relativity theory becomes important where unimaginable speed is concerned, so quantum mechanics helps to explain events arising when dealing with almost inconceivably small entities." (Quantum theory and the theory of relativity mark the study of physics at its furthest extremes. Their conclusions don't exactly replace the laws of classical Newtonian physics; those laws still hold in the overwhelming majority of cases most of us encounter. But in certain circumstances, quantum theory and the theory of relativity are the best tools of understanding available.)

When You Want to Change the Subject...

As with the Theory of Relativity, odds are high that your conversational partner will have no idea how to discuss this subject intelligently, which leaves you with any number of options. You might decide to make the point that the act of observing the speed of an electron alters the very situation being observed in a fundamental way—and then introduce your own thoughts on perception and participation relevant to, say, philosophy or sculpture. (*See separate entries:* "Philosophy" and "Sculptured.")

Words to the Wise

Quantum theory is full of paradoxes that some of the great scientific minds of history have had a devil of a time reconciling. Beware of making broad, blanket statements about waves, particles, or pretty much anything else.

HOW TO IMPRESS ANYBODY ABOUT

Religion

The dictionary defines religion as, "A system of belief to which a social group is committed, and in which an object of worship or a prescribed code of ethics may assume great importance." So—now that we've clarified *that,* we can move on without dealing with any of the pesky specifics, right? Because people tend to get *really* offended when you oversimplify or misstate aspects of their religion, and you wouldn't want to take a chance on doing that, would you? What's that you say? You're feeling brave? You actually want to develop a working acquaintance with the tenets and practices of the world's most influential faiths?

Okay. From here on out you're on your own. Write me no nasty letters about what follows. Use it with great care, and understand that it's meant to offer a *condensed summary* of key points. And remember that a truly openminded question will help you build more bridges than an accusatory listing of differences between your faith and someone else's.

The Straight Scoop

Note that any listing of "major" religions implies that those that are not listed are somehow "minor"—not a good point from which to begin. So let's just say that the summaries that follow focus on the five *most prominent* global religions—those that have made their influence felt in a wide variety of cultural settings.

Buddhism was founded about 525 B.C. by Siddhartha Gautama, also known as the Buddha, who reached a state of enlightenment thanks to a long period of meditation. His religion emphasizes the use of bodily and spiritual discipline to attain freedom from the physical world. The Buddhist's aim is to attain nirvana, a word that can be loosely translated as a condition of total tranquility in which the practitioner is completely liberated from distractions and deluded thoughts of the self. Sacred texts include the *Tripitaka,* an assemblage of teachings of the Buddha. There is also a large collection of Buddha's sayings and expositions, many of which are known as sutras. There are three main divisions within Buddhism: Theravada (the only remnant of the traditional Hinayana schools), which highlights the importance of purity in mental process and deeds; Mahayana, which includes the Zen and Soka-Gakkai schools and encompasses a broad range of philosophical and spiritual practices, some of which emphasize ideas of grace; and Tantrism, an eclectic gathering of beliefs centered on ritual and meditation. These divisions are actually of limited use, because Buddhist practice and doctrine vary widely by sect and region. There is remarkable variety within the religion. Some core principles, however, guide virtually all Buddhists: life is suffering and decay and is not essentially real; a cycle of birth and death persists because of desire and a delusive attachment to a perceived "self"; right action and right meditation can conclude the cycle and allow the practitioner to attain the liberation inherent in the nothingness of nirvana.

Christianity is a varied grouping of traditions with global reach; despite their remarkable variety, all Christian denominations are founded on the ministry, death, and resurrection of Jesus Christ, as recounted in the Gospels of the New Testament. The fundamental Christian doctrine is that humanity is saved, and its sins forgiven, by the grace of God through Christ; practitioners anticipate and celebrate new, eternal life in fellowship with one another. It's impossible to detail all the practices and beliefs of the many Christian denominations in a book like this, but you can certainly learn enough to impress others, most of whom will know less. It's worth noting that the Roman Catholic church traces its founding directly to Jesus himself, and accords a special authority to the pope; that the Orthodox church, of equally ancient origin, was originally the eastern wing of the traditional Christian church until it broke with the Roman wing in 1054, after many years of disagreement over doctrine and authority; and that the extraordinarily diverse group of Protestant denominations arose after the Reformation of the sixteenth century, and now features a truly remarkable array of sects (over two hundred!), both new and old. Major Protestant traditions include Baptists, the Church of Christ (Disciples), Episcopalians, Jehovah's Witnesses, Latter-Day Saints (Mormons), Lutherans, Methodists, Presbyterians, and members of the United Church of Christ. In recent years, an ecumenical movement, seeking to emphasize common points of observance and belief among Christians, has gained increasing momentum.

Hinduism is a religion of ancient and imperfectly understood origins with no single founder. It arose in about 1500 B.C. when the Vedic practices of Aryan invaders mingled with the existing practices of indigenous peoples in India. It is made up of countless sects and has no formal ecclesiastical structure. There are, however, certain core beliefs, including: acceptance of Vedic scriptures as sacred; the existence of a single divine principle expressed in the form of many gods; and reverence for life itself as a sacred aspect of divine unity. At the same time, Hindus acknowledge that the cycle of birth, death, and rebirth (*samsara*) is, under the principle of karma, governed by the deeds of an individual in his or her previous incarnations. To attain freedom from past misdeeds, by means of purification of the self and selfless devotion to any of the numerous divine incarnations, is, within Hinduism, of paramount importance. The faith has been marked by a seemingly limitless number of deities and regional practices—and also by a strong association with the caste system, which has historically positioned certain hereditary groups above or below other groups. (A number of aspects of the caste system have been reformed in the twentieth century, but resistance to fundamental change has often been resolute in India.) Although primarily identified with India, Hinduism has had a profound influence on other faiths—particularly Buddhism, which grew out of it.

Islam was founded by the Prophet Muhammad in Medina, on the Arabian peninsula, in 622 A.D. Its sacred text is the Koran (which is considered, in its original, untranslated form, to be the definitive word of God); also of vital importance are the *Hadith,* collections of sayings traditionally ascribed to the Prophet. Followers of Islam are known as Muslims; they have five duties. Those duties are: 1) to make a profession of faith ("There is no God but Allah ..."); 2) to pray five times daily; 3) to render a certain amount of one's worldly wealth to charity; 4) to fast during daylight hours of the holy month of Ramadan; and 5) to make, if possible, the holy pilgrimage to Mecca. Islam is divided into two major sects, Sunni and Shia. The Sunni, or orthodox, school is by far the larger of the two; it encompasses a broad spectrum of belief and practice, but can be distinguished from the Shia school by its conviction that religious guidance should proceed primarily from the Koran and Hadith—rather than human spiritual leaders—and by its generally staid and deterministic approach to matters of religious conduct. Shiite Muslims emphasize free will in a way that Sunnis do not, and accord great importance to the succession of perfect teachers known as imams. A third important tradition is the mystical Sufi movement, which emphasizes the believer's direct experience of the divine. Islam is rigorously monotheistic; it shares many common elements with Judaism and Christianity.

Judaism was founded around 1300 B.C. Although the patriarch Abraham is considered to be the founder of this religion, the Torah serves as the fundamental source of its teachings. The written Torah—the first five books of the Hebrew Bible—is regarded as sacred; also seen as inspired are the Talmud, the Midrash, the remaining books of the Hebrew Bible (which are generally used as the Old Testament by the Roman Catholic Church), and a large number of additional commentaries. Dietary restrictions and observance of the Jewish sabbath are matters of great importance. The three main contemporary branches—Orthodox, Conservative, and Reform—reflect an extraordinary diversity of practice, with the Reform school the most accommodating to modern social influences, and the Orthodox school the most committed to the maintenance of ancient practices and observances. Even within these schools, there are varying points of view concerning the degree and manner that scriptural obligations should influence the day-to-day lives of practicing Jews. Some core beliefs unite all practitioners: There is a single God, the creator and king of the universe, who established a special relationship with the Hebrew people and established divine law to regulate their affairs. In obeying the dictates of God, practicing Jews regard themselves as serving as an extraordinary witness to divine mercy. Practitioners within Judaism generally place a heavy emphasis on the importance of ethical behavior toward others; this is coupled, in traditional congregations, with a commitment to observe ritual obligations of long standing.

What You Can Say

Let's face it. When it comes to religion, your best bet is simply to quote the masters. Don't go out of your way to antagonize anyone; don't make broad generalizations; don't start making parallels that you won't be able to back up. Just smile and say, "Wasn't it so-and-so who said ... "

Here are some words to live by from people who knew exactly what it took to live by words to live by:

"I feel that there is a God, and I do not feel that there is none. For me that is enough." (Jean de la Bruyère)

"All evil vanishes from life for him who keeps the sun in his heart." (Ramayana)

"If you have love you will do all things well." (Thomas Merton)

"Religion is doing; a man does not merely think his religion, or feel it, he 'lives' his religion as much as he is able, otherwise it is not a religion but fantasy or philosophy." (George Gurdjieff)

"God is day and night, winter and summer, war and peace, surfeit and hunger." (Heraclitus)

"God is a circle whose center is everywhere and circumference nowhere." (Voltaire)

When You Want to Change the Subject...

... just start breathing deeply and gazing off into the infinite while your conversational partner gets worked into some theological dither or other. When a lull presents itself, simply say, "My (uncle/father/sainted gray-haired grandmother—whatever) always used to say that the best religion is always your own sense of purpose. I guess that's the best yardstick I've come up with yet. Now, on a more secular note..."

Words to the Wise

When in doubt, remember the virtue of silence

HOW TO IMPRESS ANYBODY ABOUT

The Renaissance

Bob Dylan once mentioned in an interview that nobody who was involved in the major social and artistic changes of the sixties thought of the period as the sixties at the time. The same principle holds true of the Renaissance—that convenient label was applied in the eighteenth century, well after the period in question had passed. What exactly, were people labeling? That's what you're about to find out.

The Straight Scoop

The Renaissance began in Italy during the early 1300s; its beginnings are generally associated with the Italian writers Petrarch and Bocaccio, with the emergence of printing technology, and with the important new voyages of exploration of this period. The Renaissance is considered to be one of the great ages of human cultural and intellectual achievement, and to divide the medieval from the modern era.

The four-century period that followed was most notable for the rediscovery of the cultures and the scholarly and artistic achievements of ancient Greece and Rome. Classical thinkers, writers, and artists were embraced by many in Europe—but there was more to the era than simply reexamining what the old guys had to say about the world. The period was characterized by an intense interest in individual literary and artistic achievement; in geographical exploration; and—perhaps most revolutionary of all—in open scientific inquiry. The long-dead Aristotle, for instance, whose work had been blindly accepted for centuries as the final authority on many scientific matters, was finally disputed by the best minds of the day on such questions as whether the planets resided within crystal spheres.

During the gradual unfolding of the Renaissance, there was a greater acceptance of the notion that a person could be significant—that the human is not eclipsed by the divine. This idea was the core assertion of the Humanist movement, which arose in the fourteenth century and was a powerful motivating force for later changes in the arts and sciences in Europe.

The changes brought about by the Renaissance—fueled, in large part, by economic shifts—were gradual, and were felt in different parts of Europe at different times. Broadly speaking, however, the "reawakening" first experienced in Italy in the fourteenth century had an extraordinary liberating effect on social, artistic, musical, scientific, and literary developments in Western European countries until about the seventeenth century. The emergence of economically based class systems was an important element in the transition.

Crucial figures of the Renaissance include the artists Leonardo da Vinci, Michelangelo di Lodovico Buonarotti, Benvenuto Cellini, and Raphael; the scientists Nicholas Copernicus, Galileo Galilei, and Johannes Kepter; the essayists Francis Bacon, Michel Eyquemde, Montaigne, and Desiderius Erasmos; the novelist Miquelde Cervantes; and the playwrights Thomas Marlowe, William Shakespeare, and Ben Jonson.

What You Can Say

"Don't you wonder whether there were days when Galileo regretted souping up that damned telescope he'd heard about?" (Galileo's persuasive publication outlining theories in support of Copernicus's heliocentric [sun-centered] model of the planetary system was banned by the Roman Catholic Church. It had been based on his own observations of the heavens through a newfangled invention, the telescope. The great scientist was threatened with torture, forced to recant his theory, and placed under house arrest in his final years.)

"How do you suppose da Vinci managed to learn to write backwards, anyway?" (Leonardo da Vinci assembled over four thousand pages of notebooks containing various diagrams and observations; much of it was written in reverse to ensure confidentiality. Da Vinci was perhaps the greatest example of the Renaissance man, in that he was an accomplished painter, engineer, scientist, and sculptor. Although many of his scientific speculations are of interest for their perceptive curiosity and their extraordinary imagination, he was not a major contributor to technological advancements undertaken during his lifetime. He was, however, an immensely influential artist and a master of composition. Leonardo da Vinci is generally regarded as one of the major figures of the Italian Renaissance, and as one of the most brilliant minds of all time.)

"The ceiling of the Sistine Chapel took Michelangelo four years; he painted it mostly on his back, looking up." (Michelangelo di Lodovico Buonarotti, strongly influenced by Leonardo da Vinci, possessed seemingly superhuman talent as a painter and sculptor; he was also a gifted poet and architect. His sculptures include such iconic works as the Pietà and David. His Biblically-themed paintings on the massive ceiling of the Sistine Chapel are an enduring monument both to human inspiration and to human endurance— and a fitting visual representation of the high aspriations and extraordinary individual achievements of the Renaissance itself.)

When You Want to Change the Subject...

Pick a favorite artist or writer of the period and focus on current discussions of that person's work and influence. (*For additional help see the entry,* "Shakespeare.")

Words to the Wise

The Renaissance was an extraordinary, and extraordinarily complex, period, but it was, in the end, supported by a single simple idea that within a society individual human beings could be important, by virtue of their humanity. "What a piece of work is a man." (Talk about your revolutionary concept!) If you get lost during the discussion, try looking for that single thread; you'll usually be able to find your way.

HOW TO IMPRESS ANYBODY ABOUT

Rock and Roll

The music of grassroots rebellion or a cynical medium notable chiefly for cannily packaged "product"? Rock and roll has been both for nearly half a century, and it's been pretty hard to miss. Here's a thinking person's review of some key points about pop culture's loudest, messiest cultural landmark—ideas you may have missed while you were doing the Hully-Gully, the Twist, the Locomotion, or the Pogo.

Note: The fact that rock and roll takes longer to describe credibly than some other topics in this book doesn't mean that it's more important than those other topics, but rather that it's occasionally more of a godforsaken, hard-to-summarize mess.

The Straight Scoop

What, exactly, is rock and roll? Perhaps the best of the (many) vaguely unsatisfying answers is that it's the contemporary music of explicit or implied rebellion.

On a technical level, rock and roll is an American hybrid musical form influenced by blues, gospel, country, and swing; it emerged in a variety of complicated local flavors in the late forties and early fifties. It was gravely condemned in its early, regional forms as a threat to the morals of young America, at which point it attained a great and enduring national popularity that it has never lost, despite some harrowing periods of inanity and uninspired self-imitation.

The rebellion factor is an important one. The music we call rock and roll was, at the outset, indistinguishable from the briskly paced, exuberant rhythm and blues that had been around for years. The music only started to take shape as an unsteady institution unto itself when white teenagers embraced the very music that had always been recorded by, and intended for, black people. In so doing, white teenagers were making an important statement of personal identity. But they were also embracing a type of music in which black listeners needed no schooling.

So it was that, in post-World War II America, the infectious, frankly sensuous appeal of the first-generation rock records started reverberating for white teens in ways that were increasingly difficult for white authority figures to ignore. White artists soon took up the cause, often delivering more accessible versions of songs that had been recorded earlier (and, purists might argue, better) by black bands. Formerly sacrosanct barriers started to fall. Companies started making very large amounts of money. Parents started to get worried. And rock and roll, which had somehow arisen in a teenhormone–driven rush in cities like Memphis, New Orleans, and Chicago more or less simultaneously, began a struggle to identify itself—a struggle that pitted the goal of mainstream acceptance against the goal of mainstream rebellion. That perpetually unresolved struggle has marked the form's extended—and probably perpetual—adolescence, which is only fitting. Rock and roll is, after all, the music of adolescence itself.

Rock and roll's only cardinal sin is boredom, and as a general rule the music has gotten boring only when its fans have failed to take up the challenge of rebelling convincingly. Fortunately, the form has usually stumbled its way into unpredicted and unpredictable infusions of fresh energy and innovation (via, for instance, early-1950s Memphis, mid-1960s San Francisco, late-1970s New York, early-1990s Seattle, and overseas booster shots too numerous to count). Rock and roll has always found ways to surprise itself, at least for a moment or two. At the same time, it has always found ways to mystify, at least for a moment or two, the faintly sulphur-scented men in business suits, limousines, or skyscrapers whose sworn duty, held far more solemnly than that of the fundamentalist preachers of the fifties, is to try to make their business predictable—and kill rock and roll for good.

What You Can Say

In the five tumultuous decades it's been on the national scene, rock and roll has seen some phenomenal rises, some gut-wrenching descents, and, most important of all, some great music. Here's an (abbreviated) quotable summary of the main, but by no means the only, keepers of the flame. Take what you want and toss it into the conversation wherever it seems to fit best.

The Fifties: Sam Phillips founds Memphis's Sun Records, the label that will debut Elvis Presley, Howlin' Wolf, B. B. King, Johnny Cash, Jerry Lee Lewis, and Ike Turner (whose much later abuse of his wife Tina will come to overshadow his role as one of rock and roll's most important pioneers). Disc jockey Alan Freed gets kids excited about the new music and launches rock's first stage show. Bill Haley shows that white guys know how to make hit rock and roll records. Presley emerges as the King. Little Richard, Chuck Berry, and Jerry Lee Lewis become major national acts. Buddy Holly's brief but influential career ends when he dies in a plane crash with Ritchie Valens and the Big Bopper on February 3, 1959—"The day the music died." But it didn't.

The Sixties: The Twist takes over America, and Chubby Checker becomes a household name. "Girl groups" (the Shangri-Las, the Shirelles, the Crystals, etc.) are all the rage; Phil Spector develops his distinctive "wall of sound" production style. The Beach Boys, most of whom don't surf, turn the West Coast surfing craze into a backdrop for a string of memorable hits. The Beatles storm the USA bearing adrenaline-laced records and screaming fans; the group establishes itself as the prototype Band That Knows Exactly What It Wants to Do Next. The subsequent "British Invasion" yields a profusion of British acts, notably the Rolling Stones and the Who, and it drums out much of the native-grown competition. Nevertheless, folk icon Bob Dylan emerges from the narrow confines of "protest music" and

embraces electric rock and roll. Motown acts (The Supremes, The
Temptations, The Miracles, et al.) stand tall. An acid-laced brand of
pleasantly incomprehensible psychedelic rock, played by acts like
Jimi Hendrix, Jefferson Airplane, and The Grateful Dead, emerges
from various corners, in particular London and San Francisco's
Haight Ashbury; at about the same time, New York's Velvet Under-
ground starts its relentless campaign to shatter preconceptions even
if it means annoying some people. The Doors (from Los Angeles) and
The MC5 (from Detroit) also startle complacent audiences in
distinctive, high-energy ways. The huge festival in Woodstock, N.Y.
essentially defines the term "letting it all hang out." (Go ahead—say
you were there. No one remembers the event precisely.) The Rolling
Stones's image as rock and roll's "bad boys" is forever solidified when
an unruly free concert in Altamont (Northern California) gets way
out of hand and culminates in a fatal stabbing.

The Seventies: The Beatles, having exemplified all that was
optimistic, synergy-driven, and creative in the previous decade,
choose early 1970 to publicly collapse into a heap of rubble. The
decade goes downhill from there; apart the ascent of a few inspired
new acts (for instance, the Allman Brothers, Led Zeppelin, glam-rock
monarch David Bowie, Lou Reed, Iggy Pop, and George Clinton's
Parliament-Funkadelic), there is, by the end of 1972, little to defend
in a rock scene that has grown complacent and self-satisfied. Several
years of vapid, danceable treacle, reminiscent of the bland "pop"
periods immediately preceding the breakthroughs of Presley and the
Beatles, follow. The punk movement, inspired by restless youths in
England disgusted with a similarly irrelevant pop scene in that
country, leads to groundbreaking, energizing, and refreshingly
unkempt work by British bands like The Sex Pistols, The Damned,
and The Clash, and American bands like The Ramones, X, and The
Cramps. As influential as the punk scene is, it doesn't make much of
a mark on the Billboard charts until the nineties.

The Eighties: ...when David Byrne's quirky, enigmatic band
Talking Heads makes it safe to dance again. Music videos emerge as
an essential means of marketing and (secondarily?) enjoying rock
and roll music. Various long-established, successful acts from bygone

years (notably the Who and the Rolling Stones) mount earnest, eerily well-financed tours, presumably to convince the world at large of their continued marketability and relevance, in that order. The Police, headed by frontman and lyricist Sting, prove that you can play intense, hypnotic rock and roll and make references to Vladimir Nabokov at the same time. Michael Jackson's *Thriller* album conquers every conceivable obstacle to super-mega-hyper-insert-superlative-of-choice hitdom, including the formerly white-artist-dominated video network MTV. Jackson's album is the subject of such ludicrous overexposure that debates over whether or not it actually qualifies as rock and roll quickly become moot. Prince (aping Little Richard and Jimi Hendrix) and Madonna (seducing legions of followers with various provocative media displays) attract huge audiences. Bruce Springsteen, hailed by many as a live-gig messiah at the close of the previous decade, strikes it big with a big-bucks, big-sound, big-tour assault on the nation's attention. At least he knows who Bob Dylan is. Inner-city rap and hip-hop acts gain in influence and depth of social insight, led by bands like Public Enemy and N.W.A. Various hair bands play an ominously predictable style of heavy-metal rock until...

The Nineties: ...Seattle erupts, and the grunge band Nirvana leads a successful, and extremely loud, assault on complacency and big-label image control. (And takes what the punk of the 70s evolved into—grunge—and puts it on the charts.) Nirvana lead singer Kurt Cobain adds his name to the long list of drug-related rock deaths; his widow, Courtney Love, presses on and leads the band Hole to messy, critically acclaimed levels of extravagance. Influences from Jamaica, Africa, India (sixties redux, anyone?), and South America are evident in a vibrant World Music scene. At home, the sounds from the 'hood grow ever more insistent. P. J. Harvey continues the good, eclectic, and satisfyingly bone-rattling job of thrashing musical and vocal boundaries, and Alanis Morissette rakes America over the coals with her distinctive, calculatedly ragged message of sexually-driven outrage. And somewhere, in a foreign or domestic garage, bedroom, or attic, someone is tuning up an old guitar and plotting the next assault on what you thought rock and roll really was.

In addition, you may wish to weigh in with the following:

"It's got an intensity that hits you right here [pound your heart]." (The all-purpose fall-back if you're challenged by some effete snob who doesn't care for your brand of rock and roll. If it moves you, it moves you. If it doesn't, it's not getting the job done.)

Or you might say, "If you're looking for a great white rock pioneer, look no further than Woody Guthrie." (Guthrie was a direct and powerful influence on Bob Dylan, and an indirect one on the Beatles, who developed more complex chord structures via the English skiffle craze of the fifties. Guthrie's music had been an important part of the skiffle fad.)

Or you might ask, "Do you know who plays the drums on 'The Ballad of John and Yoko?'" (The answer: Paul McCartney. Ringo was unavailable at the time. Paul also played drums on "Back in the U.S.S.R.")

When You Want to Change the Subject…

… turn up the music to 11 and let it speak for itself.

Words to the Wise

Any discussions you may happen to hold with actual aging rock stars may seem a trifle one-sided. There are a number of possible reasons for this:

- The rock star is avoiding you
- The rock star is experiencing a drug-related flashback
- The rock star is deaf
- The rock star is praying you'll talk about investment strategies rather than rebellion

Take your pick and improvise accordingly… or move on to someone else.

The Roman Empire

Complete the following sentences:

> "All roads lead to ..."
> "When in ..."
> "... wasn't built in a day."

If you guessed Hackensack, Peoria, or Oakland, you're laboring under a serious conversational handicap when it comes to the greatest metropolis of antiquity, and will no doubt benefit from what follows. Rome was the first great global city; it grew from a modest settlement centered on seven small hills near the Tiber River to become the seat of a massive empire—the most far-reaching the world had yet seen—of several million square miles. If you think New York was the original City That Never Sleeps, consider the observation of the satirist Juvenal, who wrote that socially prominent, economically active Roman citizens "can scarce afford to sleep"—predating their present-day Manhattan imitators by many centuries.

The Straight Scoop

According to legend, Rome was founded in 753 B.C. by the orphan twins Romulus and Remus, on the banks of the Tiber. The twins, the legend held, had been the offspring of the vestal virgin Rhea Silvia and the god Mars; they had been set adrift on the Tiber by the usurping king of Alba Longa, Amulius. The basket in which they had been placed made it to land, and the two were suckled by a she-wolf, and raised by a royal shepherd and his wife. After restoring their grandfather, Numitor, the true king, to his throne, the twins returned to the spot where they had been rescued on the Tiber and founded a new city.

After that, things got complicated, as they often would in Roman politics in the centuries to come. The two brothers argued, and Romulus slew Remus.

We can now leave the legendary material and note with historical confidence that Rome was ruled by a series of foreign kings until 509 B.C., when the Roman Republic was established. It lasted for over four centuries. Rome was then governed by two elected consuls—patricians only—who were advised by a senate. The Republic was not a democracy at any point in its development; modern historical and political experts are inclined to define it as a patrician aristocracy at its outset and a senatorial oligarchy at its conclusion. It is true, however, that Rome popularly elected assemblies gradually (and even sneakily) assumed legislative powers once retained by the consuls. By the third century B.C., the senate had attained complete primacy over the consuls, but tensions between patricians and plebians remained important forces in Roman politics. All the same, Rome's ascent toward world dominance had begun.

The Roman Republic was a model for balanced government, but it was not to endure. The rule of the popular and able military hero Julius Caesar—who had both defeated his former ally Pompey and significantly expanded Rome's already astonishing geographical reach—marked the final phase of the Republic. Caesar's rule had been the culmination of a long series of dictators and strongmen representing competing political factions. The truth was that the old system had been rendered unstable; the demands of governing far-flung regions proved too much for the senatorial system.

Caesar made shrewd (and successful) attempts to govern by means of existing institutions. All the same, his capable administration, which marked a high point in Roman history and culture, placed a single, dominant leader at the center of the government, and set the stage for the long period of empire that was to follow. Caesar was assassinated in 44 B.C. A period of political turmoil followed, culminating in the emergence of the Second Triumvirate, composed of Caesar's ward and grandnephew, Octavian (later to be known as Augustus), Marc Antony, and Lepidus. (The First Triumvirate, which had consisted of Julius Caesar, Pompey, and Crassus, had been formed in 60 B.C.)

Like its predecessor, the Second Triumvirate did not endure; Octavian defeated Antony and Cleopatra at Actium in 31 B.C., and received the title Augustus Caesar from the Senate. Augustus, aware of the taint attached to monarchy for the Romans, was careful to observe traditional political forms—but exercised ultimate power. He is usually regarded as the first of the Roman emperors. His was a remarkable reign, one that featured intelligent organization of the military and the provincial governments, the development of an extraordinary network of roads connecting the Empire's distant outposts, and the official patronage of great artists and writers. Augustus's reign initiated the long phase known as the Pax Romana—the Roman Peace. The Empire would be ruled by a series of emperors until its fall—but none would prove as effective a leader as Augustus.

Through conquest and colonization, by the second century A.D., the Roman Empire had a population of fifty to seventy million people on three continents. At its height, the Empire controlled all of present-day Italy, half of Europe, much of the Middle East, and the north coast of Africa.

In 395 A.D., the Empire was permanently split into Eastern and Western halves, with the Eastern portion emerging as the Byzantine Empire. Rome was no longer the world's preeminent political force. In 476 A.D. the Western Empire, weakened by repeated invasions and unable to govern its vast empire, fell to Germanic tribes, but this event merely confirmed decades of political decline.

Ancient Rome, itself strongly influenced by the Greeks, had extraordinary effects on the development of Western civilization. Its culture and many of its institutions shaped some of the most important governments and institutions of the eras that followed (such as the Roman Catholic Church, and the U.S. Constitution). Among the most enduring legacies of the Romans were their political institutions; their outstanding technological advancements in roadways, construction, and waterworks; their unmistakable architecture; their hugely influential literature; and their language, the precursor of modern tongues. Romance languages such as French, Spanish, and Italian. (English, too, has of course been strongly influenced by Latin, but it is not directly derived from it).

What You Can Say

"The uppercase letters we read are essentially the same ones the Romans were reading in 600 B.C." (Lowercase letters didn't come along until 300 A.D.)

"The brilliant Roman lawyer Cicero perfected many legal defense techniques still used today." (For instance, he was an expert at savaging the opposition during his oration in order to take attention off his client—the ancient equivalent of O. J. Simpson attorney Johnny Cochran putting the police on trial.)

"The founding fathers used Republican Rome as one model for their blueprint for constitutional government." (The American idea that separate, legitimate branches of government could coexist relatively harmoniously, rather than compete for definitive primacy, was in part the result of careful study of what had and hadn't worked in Roman history.)

"Did you ever wonder why the Romans put so many water fountains in their cities?" (These were planned by Roman hydraulic engineers, to relieve pressure on pipes from the momentum of water traveling downhill.)

You should also be ready to discuss some of the most important emperors. Here are some thumbnail sketches of some who followed Augustus:

Tiberius: Augustus's stepson; he assumed leadership when Augustus died in 14 A.D. He held fast to most of Augustus's policies, but initiated some fiscally prudent but unpopular belt-tightening at home when he cut back on luxury costs (such as public spectacles). Tiberius's general Germanicus Caesar stopped a military rebellion following Augustus's death, and waged war in Germany. Though not well regarded by Roman historians, Tiberius is now thought by many to have been a capable administrator. He was certainly more stable than ...

Caligula: His rule began in 37 A.D. It was initially supported by the military, and it was nothing if not interesting. Caligula quickly emerged as one of history's supreme tyrants; he was a cruel, mentally unstable autocrat with an unquenchable thirst for torture, execution, and depravity. Leaving aside for the moment his lewdness, violence, self-aggrandizement, and consistently bizarre behavior, Caligula was a loose cannon as an administrator, a man with little sense of the practical political consequences of his acts. (His attempt to raise a statue of himself in the Jewish temple in Palestine, for instance, very nearly started a rebellion.) And yes, it's true that he named his horse Incitatus to the consulship. Caligula was assassinated in 41 A.D., after only four years as emperor, by a tribune of the Praetorian Guard. Caligula was succeeded by ...

Claudius: Tiberius's nephew; he was an accomplished scholar, a serious historian, and a competent administrator. Of course, nearly *anyone* would have looked good after Caligula, but Claudius's accomplishments during the years of his reign (41–54 A.D.) are hard to deny. The empire itself was extended significantly while he ruled. Claudius was lame and had a speech impediment, and was ridiculed mercilessly for these defects in his early life. He is, in modern times, one of the best-known Roman emperors, thanks to the two popular Robert Graves books about him and the later Public Television series based on those books. He was poisoned (according to the historian Tacitus) by his fourth wife, Agrippina the Younger, and was succeeded by ...

Nero: Claudius's stepson, but more reminiscent in some ways of Caligula, in that he is believed to have murdered his own mother, Agrippira (yes, the same woman who allegedly poisoned Claudius),

Claudius's son Britannicus, two wives, and a whole lot of other people. Half of Rome was consumed by a fire in 64 A.D.; Nero accused Christians of starting the blaze and began a ruthless persecution of the sect. Later, he launched a similarly murderous campaign against his own political enemies. In 68 A.D. a military revolt led to his suicide. Nero thought highly of his own abilities as an actor and singer; his last words included the lament, "What an artist the world is losing in me!"

When You Want to Change the Subject...

Point out that ancient Rome's standard of living was extraordinarily high—with the wealthy enjoying such amenities as running water and central heating—and would not be matched for over a thousand years in European cities. Wonder aloud how the ancient Romans, while not miracle-workers, were able to care, at public expense, for the two hundred thousand poverty-stricken who lived in the city, and ask for opinions on whether modern American society will ever be able to meet this high standard.

Words to the Wise

The emperors whose reigns are summarized above are only the first four to follow Augustus. Constantine the Great (306–337) divided the empire and made Christianity the official religion; Justinian (ruler of the eastern empire or Byzantine, 527–565) codified Roman law and profoundly influenced legal history.

Sculpture

Sculpted forms have been found in some of the earliest discovered human settlements: small animals, voluptuous female forms, and, eventually, what appear to be small toys with wheels and game pieces. From mud pies to silly putty, fashioning stuff out of other stuff is an inherently human activity. The youngest child loves the feel of modeling clay, and, given the chance, will start to shape it more or less instantly. And even the busiest executive may bend and shape a paper clip during a meeting.

But what does it all *mean?* And how can you talk about it intelligently?

The Straight Scoop

The important thing to remember about sculpture is that the sculptor is, as a rule, an active participant in the piece. He or she is likely to meditate deeply on the task at hand before making that first strike, perhaps in an effort to free the inner sprit of the materials—or perhaps because cash constraints mean there's only one big piece of marble and the sculptor doesn't want to blow it. The sculptor literally shapes the outcome of the piece, for better or worse. One tap too many, and that "Winged Victory" won't take flight in quite the way anyone had in mind.

The Greeks called their statues of men *kouroi* (singular *kouros*, meaning "young man"). These were highly stylized figures of compact men. They exhibited what we call closed form. (No holes or hollow places.) The Greeks created these sturdy, direct works in the image of the perfect male—which, to them, was the ideal subject. Once Greece reached its golden era of art, science, and government (about 600 B.C.), sculptural experiments and refinements had been made. Figures began to take on a more relaxed shape, and sculptures seemed to (literally) open up—gaps appeared, sometimes in apparent defiance of gravity. A knee would bend, or an arm might hold a bunch of grapes. The Greeks even started making more figures of women. This period gave rise to open form (occasional holes and hollow places).

These works exuded an aura of awe and respect, primarily because the specially chosen subjects were considered worthy of reverence by just about everyone in the community. But in the world of art, ancient or modern, it is often the patron who calls the shots, and soon anybody who was anybody was going out and having his statue or bust (a work displaying a figure from the shoulders up) carved. "Hey, if you're gonna make a nice figure of Aphrodite for the temple, how about one of me, the guy who made it all possible? I think it would look great right over there, in the town square."

In the Middle Ages, it was more likely that the Church was doing the paying, so if you wanted to be a sculptor you had to brush up on your saints and angels. Call this the Gothic age and keep in mind that the figures being represented were still ones that contained power, right down to the last little protective gargoyle (a pagan image, by the way). With all the cathedrals being built, there was lots and lots of work to be had. Much of the best decorative sculpture at this time was done through the use of bas relief (a form carved as part of a wall or other flat surface that may give the illusion of depth). Sculptors often went into great detail on a very large scale, which is another way of saying that they were giving their ecclesiastical patrons their money's worth. "Okay, Giuseppe—we need something nice for the big empty spot over that door, just past that flying buttress."

A line of famous sculptors working in a wide variety of forms and styles (Donatello de Betto di Bardi, Lorenzo Ghiberti, Michelangelo di Lodovico Buonarotti) emerged during the Italian Renaissance, particularly in Florence. Michelangelo's famous *David* is considered one of the triumphs of the period. Later, the great architect and sculptor Giovanni Lorenzo Bernini, the towering figure of the Italian Baroque period, executed pieces of staggering technical mastery and drama, often with pronounced religious themes.

A more secular variety of royally sponsored sculpture emerged in some parts of Europe (notably France) in the sixteenth and seventeenth centuries. Suddenly, it seemed that everybody was sculpting like mad and focusing on new themes, freeing their work and giving rise to a bewildering variety of schools, movements, and countermovements.

Then, in the twentieth century, just as it seemed as if things couldn't get more complicated, along came Marcel Duchamp and the Dada school. Dada is a nonsense word Duchamp and his friends used to make people ask, "What is Art?" and similarly provocative questions. Duchamp was the one who thought it would be fun to put a urinal in a big exhibition and call it *Fountain*. Duchamp and his "Readymades" (everyday objects) continued to challenge boundaries and upset logical applecarts in precisely the way they were intended to. Later on, he mounted a show that consisted of elaborately constructed machines that served no function. Much of the twentieth-century sculpture that followed—with its obsession over questions of form and function, its renegade sensibility, and its elusive emotional appeal—took its cue from Duchamp and his eyebrow-raising Dada friends. One can imagine them pausing at a modern museum's water cooler and declaring it to be the best part of the exhibit.

In our day, the assemblage artist Christo has seemingly gone Duchamp one better by transforming everyday objects, typically by wrapping them up. He started small, with motorcycles and the like, then worked his way up to whole buildings, and eventually appropriated a 24 mile-long chunk of California by erecting a temporary white "running fence," a sweeping and quite beautiful installation that challenged, yet again, prevailing notions of what sculpture could and couldn't be.

What You Can Say

Lines of conversation to consider including in your discussions of sculpture, old or new:

"The real magic in sculpture comes with grasping that the object stands with us as an active participant; we help to bring it into being." (You may or may not get challenged on this one. If you are, proceed to...)

"Does a free standing work exist in three dimensions at once?" (Most would agree that it must, but the viewer can only see the image from one side at a time. So in some ways the objects exist in time, as well—a fourth dimension—as the viewer becomes an active participant in the object. The viewer walks around the piece, seeing it from each of its sides, while moving through time.)

"Does a kinetic work imply a balance, a sense of control and continuity, that we ourselves can't really expect from modern life?" (One of the major movements in twentieth-century sculpture has been toward mobiles and other pieces that move, either when influenced by the observer or set into motion by a machine. Alexander Calder is perhaps the most famous kinetic sculptor of recent years.)

When You Want to Change the Subject...

...you might venture an opinion about the possibility that, in rendering a sculpture, an artist sets free energies or perspectives somehow already residing in the materials chosen. With a little careful nudging on your part, the discussion is now likely to move into the realm of spirituality.

Words to the Wise

You may want to brush up on your museum comportment. See the advice that appears in the section on painting.

HOW TO IMPRESS ANYBODY ABOUT

Shakespeare

Having trouble remembering your notes from that English Lit class? Here's our streamlined, *Cliff Notes* version of how to hold your own in a discussion of the Bard and impress others with the depth of your culture.

The Straight Scoop

William Shakespeare (1564–1616) is widely considered the world's greatest dramatist. His body of stage work was immensely popular in Elizabethan and Jacobean England, and it's immensely popular today, four hundred or so years later, despite the fact that the English language has undergone radical changes since the Bard of Avon's day, and many of Shakespeare's phrases now sound archaic. (Helpful hint: Shakespearean English, even in convoluted passages, is a great deal easier to understand when it's delivered out loud, with feeling, than it is when read quietly to oneself.)

Take a moment now to learn the basics of a few of Shakespeare's plays.

Hamlet: A brilliant, tortured prince seeks to avenge his murdered father.

King Lear: An old king, deceived by externals, exiles a daughter who loves him, divides his kingdom between his other two flattering daughters, and then endures humiliation and madness.

Macbeth: An ambitious nobleman, spurred on by his wife, murders the king and assumes the throne himself—but is eventually overcome, despite some misleading prophecies he hears from a band of witches.

Henry V: A shrewd, brave king defeats the French despite overwhelming odds against him.

Much Ado About Nothing: The verbal battle of the sexes rages, a virtuous young woman is slandered, and men and women decide, once everything's sorted out, that they're probably happier with each other than without.

Romeo and Juliet: Young love is tragically foiled, and the audience gets to hear some exquisite poetry.

A Midsummer Night's Dream: Young lovers get mixed up in the forest, reality and imagination get even more mixed up, and the audience gets to hear some more exquisite poetry.

Antony and Cleopatra: Mature love is tragically foiled, and the audience gets to hear still more exquisite poetry.

The Tempest: A sorcerer on an enchanted island reclaims his lost dukedom, and the poetry shoots into another dimension altogether.

Purists will insist that no short summaries can possibly do justice to these works, and they're right. Some of them will also claim that Shakespeare was a special kind of writer, a literary god whose every line is worthy of awe and reverence. They're wrong.

It's simplistic and inaccurate to think of Shakespeare as a conduit of uninterrupted literary perfection. He was a busy man of the theater who frequently had to work against some very tight deadlines. His job was to create new plays for a professional London company that was constantly hungry for new material. It's worth remembering, for the sake of perspective, that Shakespeare wrote some bad plays, too—or, at least, plays that are unlikely, on their own merits, to move a contemporary audience. He was a writer of his own time and place, not ours, which means that lots of material that made perfect sense to the Elizabethans (such as the forced conversion to Christianity of the predictably miserly Jew Shylock in *The Merchant of Venice*) rubs twentieth-century audiences the wrong way.

The quality of Shakespeare's writing is usually strong enough to ensure that even plays that don't exactly qualify as masterpieces have something to recommend them. All the same, anyone who tells you that every word Shakespeare ever wrote was inspired hasn't sat through a production of *King John, The Two Gentlemen of Verona,* or *Timon of Athens.*

For the most part, though, people are not that interested in the (small!) group of Shakespeare's works with serious structural or plotting problems. As is only natural, we're fascinated by the plays—the lines, the scenes, the characters—that work. And there is certainly no shortage of things that work in Shakespeare. Why do they move us? Ten thousand different critics might offer ten thousand different answers, some of them quite long-winded. For my part, I'll hazard a theory that takes up a bare three sentences—ready?

Shakespeare's plays (more so than his poems) move audiences around the world and across the centuries because he has a masterful way, in his best works, of refusing to take sides. His primary genius lies not in language or the building of interest in the plot, although he's a master at both, but in fooling us into thinking we've heard his side of the story. Shakespeare uses people to make compelling cases for certain points of view, and he's so persuasive that he often fools us into thinking that what we've just heard represents his own point of view, when what he's actually illustrating is more likely to be the richness of human experience.

What You Can Say

After saying what follows, you may want to try pointing out that you saw a production of the play (preferably in a faraway city some years ago) that "cut the text to ribbons" and "missed every key point of resonance in a misguided attempt to appeal to television-age audiences."

Romeo and Juliet

Famous line: "What's in a name? That which we call a rose by any other name would smell as sweet."

Modern attempt at a subtitle: *Forbidden Love and Its Consequences.* (You may want to point out that the hit Broadway musical *West Side Story* was based on Shakespeare's classic.)

"An early tragedy that's probably most effective when it focuses on young love, a theme we associate with the comedies."

A Midsummer Night's Dream

Famous line: "The Lunatic, the lover, and the poet are of imagination all compact [made up]."

Modern attempt at a subtitle: *Lovers Get Mixed Up, Higher Powers Straighten Them Out.*

"This play and *The Tempest* both show us beings who operate in otherworldly realms, guiding the action of flawed humans at key points."

Much Ado about Nothing

Famous line: "When I said I would die a bachelor, I did not think I should live till I were married."

Modern attempt at a subtitle: *Boys Will Be Boys. Girls Will Marry Them Anyway.*

"The Beatrice-and-Benedick subplot is what we remember, more so than the dark conspiracy against Hero that nearly succeeds. Maybe that's because Beatrice and Benedick are what we most want to remember."

Henry V

Famous line: "Once more into the breach, dear friends."

Modern attempt at a subtitle: *Deals with Traitors, Wins War, Gets Girl, Needs to Work on His French.*

"Henry's bungling attempts in the last act to woo the French Princess Katherine in her native tongue show that this consummate warrior and leader of men is willing even to look foolish to attain his aims."

Hamlet

Famous line: "Something is rotten in the state of Denmark."
Modern attempt at a subtitle: *Never Do Today What You Can Put Off Till Tomorrow.*

"In a story about testing, ruminating, and delaying, the four-hour-long script itself seems to hesitate to deliver its plot points until the last possible moment."

Macbeth

Famous line: "Out, out, damn'd spot."
Modern attempt at a subtitle: *Attractive Short-Term Career Move Has Its Drawbacks.*

"By murdering the king, Macbeth commits the ultimate crime, and he knows it. Shakespeare makes him pay not only by losing his life—dying is actually a respite when it comes—but by having to watch as his own psyche self-destructs."

When You Want to Change the Subject...

...mention that Shakespeare was a pragmatic writer of his era—and a popular entertainer, first and foremost. Point out what many Shakespeare fans forget: What appears to be the Bard's first early hit (*Titus Andronicus*) was the equivalent of a modern slasher film. Then ask which of the current movies in theatrical release your conversational partner could imagine Shakespeare taking on writing duties for. There! You're talking about current cinema!

Words to the Wise

Every once in a while, you'll run into someone who says that Shakespeare did not write the works attributed to him. If you find yourself trapped in a conversation with anyone who feels this way, you have two options. You can mention that some of the most respected scholars in the world have looked at all the evidence and concluded that there's absolutely nothing of merit in the various conspiracy theories. This has the advantage of being true, but the disadvantage of being likely to inspire your conversational partner to launch an impassioned debate in favor of some pet theory. If you don't feel up to this (and I certainly wouldn't blame you if you don't) you may want to explore option two: Simply smile, admit that the issue is certainly a complex one, and then leave the matter undecided by saying, "Well, the works stands on its own, whoever wrote it." This keeps you from having to comment directly on the Francis Bacon-Queen Elizabeth-Earl of Oxford-Lee Harvey Oswald stuff.

The Solar System and the Universe Beyond

Let's face it—for most of their history, human beings have had some remarkably diverse ideas about how the universe was formed, how it works, and where our own world fits in the grand (and I do mean grand) scheme of things. Not all of these ideas have been completely accurate! Only in the last century or so have we started to develop a knowledge of the physical structure of the cosmos that holds up to any rigorous analysis.

There have been any number of theories about how the universe was assembled. Most of them found some way to put human beings at the center of everything—which is, I suppose, where we imagine, at some level, we belong. The ancient Greeks held that a group of crystal spheres circulated around the earth, and that the earth's moon resided in one of these spheres. The stars were believed to occupy the farthest sphere from earth. Pretty simple, right?

That poetically balanced vision held sway until the Middle Ages. In the 1500s, Nicholas Copernicus, a gifted Polish astronomer, put forth a heliocentric (literally, "sun in the middle") theory of planetary motion—the first modern European to do so. He made the mistake of assuming that the planets must move in perfect circles, which left key mathematical questions unresolved. Many rejected the theory on what appeared to be "common sense" grounds. The sun holds still? What an absurd notion! You can *see* the thing moving every day, right?

In the following century, the Italian scientist Galileo Galilei used a telescope to analyze heavenly bodies, and discovered some pesky details that left the whole spheres-within-spheres theory looking a little shaky. The Milky Way, for instance. All of a sudden, it wasn't a single band of whitish material, but a collection of thousands upon thousands of stars—far more stars than people had been able to count with the naked eye. So the question arose: What if some stars were actually *farther away* than other stars? And what if the spheres-of-stars models turned out to be, well, a little too far out to explain what was showing up on lenses?

Galileo eventually ran into trouble with Church authorities, thanks to all that heretical talk of his about the earth revolving around the sun. (Copernicus, it turned out, had gotten the sun-in-the-center part right. Who knew?) Galileo had nevertheless opened the door for a fuller examination of the vast spaces that surround our own world, and he'd set the stage for wave after wave of intriguing questions that would continue for decades—and centuries—to come, long after his tussle with the theory had faded into the dark—really dark—past. Science, after all, has a way of holding still for no one. And eventually the question arose: What if the Milky Way weren't just any old irregularly formed stretch of stars—but the group of stars to which our solar system belongs, seen from the inside looking out?

By the 1920s, modern telescopes had demonstrated the existence of millions of stars and other galaxies far away from the Milky Way—and twentieth-century astronomers began to get some sense of the overwhelming size and complexity of the physical universe.

The Straight Scoop

Here are direct, comprehensible definitions of some of the most common terms you're likely to run into during a discussion of the great-big, wide-open spaces that extend beyond the earth's atmosphere:

Big Bang: As of this writing, this is the most widely accepted theory of the way the universe came into existence; it holds that the universe started out as something similar to a massive blast that caused all the components of the universe to move away from the center where the explosion began. This process is also known as the expanding universe phenomenon, and it has been documented by scientific observation. There's more evidence backing up the Big Bang: cosmic background radiation seems to come from all directions, and shows characteristics that are consistent with a single massive explosion from a point of infinite density (called a singularity).

Binary star: Nearly half of the stars we can see are in fact pairs of stars in orbit with one another. Scientists are occasionally able to make out both stars with powerful telescopic equipment, but more often they determine that a star is one of a binary pair as a result of the dimmer star's gravitational pull on the brighter star.

Black hole: A common, but little-understood, element of modern parlance, black hole is a heavenly body that possesses so much mass for its size that nothing—including light—can manage freeing itself from the resulting gravitional pull. The result: fantastically dense collapsed star. (Imagine the entire sun in a shotglass.) These bodies had been theorized as far back as the late eighteenth-century by astronomers who could see no other explanation for a variety of bizarre celestial anomalies. Because they don't exactly stand out in space, black holes can only be observed by their effect on their surroundings. Black holes are thought to reside at the center of a number of galaxies. One of them is our own Milky Way. In recent years, some scientists have finally declared themselves satisfied that black holes do in fact exist.

Dwarfs: These are small stars (comparatively speaking, of course) that come in different colors. The brightest dwarfs are white; the dimmest are brown. White dwarfs are stars with cores that have collapsed, and whose atoms are tightly compressed. A teaspoonful of matter from a white dwarf would weigh in at a hefty five tons. We insignificant human beings tend to think of the sun (in actuality, a star) as being, well, pretty darn big. Truth be told, though, it's only average as stars go. (See *giants* below.)

Galaxies: These are huge systems made up of very large numbers of stars, stars that are typically separated from each other by stretches of ...nothing. In the eighteenth century, an astronomer named William Herschel determined that various cloudy patches visible between stars were in fact huge systems containing billions and billions of stars. These systems only *seemed* like misty areas between familiar stars, Herschel argued, because they were located at such immense distances from the earth. Twentieth-century hardware proved that Herschel was right. The cloudlike groups he observed are today referred to as galaxies. Considering how far ahead of the pack Herschel was, it would seem only fair to refer to these groups of stars as Herschels, rather than galaxies, but I digress. The galaxy that includes our sun is, of course, known to astronomers as the Milky Way—but it's not the only, or the most impressive, specimen out there. Modern astronomers, armed with telescopic power that would make Herschel drool with envy, have learned that galaxies tend to fall into three main categories—spiral, elliptical, and irregular. Your average spiral galaxy (like the Milky Way) looks like a flat disk with a bulge, or nucleus, in the middle, that contains old stars, and with newer stars (along with gas and dust) winding around the outer portion in spiral arms. Elliptical galaxies (among which are the very largest galaxies yet observed) look pretty much like the bulge in the middle of spiral galaxies; no arms, though. Irregular galaxies don't have any apparent structure.

Giants: Big, big, big stars. Red giants are stars that have expended their core hydrogen fuel and gotten bigger about the waistline as a result. New fusion reactions start in the core, and the result is a new wave of energy that expands the helium and hydrogen outside the core; because the outer (visible) layer is comparatively cool, it is red—like the red of heated metal. If you've ever wondered what the final fate of the earth is going to be, you can stop wondering. Our sun will remain in its current state for about five billion more years (it's about four and a half billion years old now). It will eventually become a red giant, expanding past the orbits of Mercury and Venus. Then it will burn the earth to a crisp. Have a nice day.

Light year: The distance light would travel over the course of a single year. If you're keeping score at home, that's 5,878 billion miles.

Nebulae: A hazy, misty, patch of light observed in space; a collection of interstellar gas and dust. Nebulae is the plural; nebula is the singular. They are not gatherings of stars; since the 1960s, astronomers have made more accurate distinctions about supposed nebulae that turned out to be galaxies. (That doesn't stop people from talking about the Great Nebula of the Andromeda constellation, however, even though what's really under discussion is a galaxy—the most distant celestial object that can be seen with the naked eye.) There are light and dark nebulae; astronomers believe that dark, high-density nebulae known as globules are in fact stars in the process of being born. Planetary nebulae—which have clear edges and look like small disks—are dying stars in the last stages of their development.

Novae: (plural for nova) are stars that seem to come out of nowhere. (Nova comes from the Latin for "new.") There isn't really any magic involved; a dim star simply gets brighter and enters the visible range—that's a nova. A *supernova* is a huge star, heading toward the final phase of its life, that explodes and experiences a dramatic increase in brightness. The supernova is perhaps the most cataclysmic of all observed astronomical events. Other novae may be the result of material of one star in a binary pair falling into the companion star, resulting in a new, higher level of luminosity.

Planets: Objects that orbit around stars, but don't generate their own light. Nine major planets orbit around our sun, the planets closest to the sun are rocky, while the ones that are furthest away are made up mostly of liquids and gases. What's that you say? You weren't paying complete attention during certain periods of your elementary school education and can't name all the planets in our solar system? Relax. I'm here to help. Our sun's in the middle—otherwise all that grief Galileo went through was a *huge* waste of time—and the first planet is Mercury. It's followed by Venus, then us, then Mars, then Jupiter, then Saturn, then Uranus, then Neptune, then Pluto. The orbits don't run in neat circles, no matter what your fourth-grade textbook, eager to save space, may have led you to believe. (The Big Nine are the major planets; asteroids that revolve around the sun are sometimes referred to as minor planets. There's an asteroid belt between Mars and Jupiter.)

What You Can Say

"We assume, of course, that the earth is about the same age as the sun." That's the guess modern scientists have brought to the table about how and when the earth came into existence. The current theory sounds something like this: The sun condensed via a huge interstellar gas cloud; when it formed, a comparatively small amount of matter was left spinning around the new formation. Some of that stuff, liquids, hunks of rock, gathered, thanks to the pull of gravity, and, as the result of a process known as accretion, developed into lumps that would eventually emerge as the earth and other planets. The bigger groups gathered mass and gravitational force, and attracted still more hunks of debris. Think of the way dust has a way of collecting into balls of varying sizes, and you'll be on your way to visualizing the way accretion is thought to have worked during this phase. Some of the debris, though, smashed into itself, and became what we now know as meteorites. Anyway, the best current estimate on our solar system's age comes in at 4.6 billion years.

"The universe, on the other hand," you can go on to say, "appears to be four or five times as old as that." Contemporary scientists estimate that the universe is between fifteen and twenty billion years old. They arrive at this figure by using the rate of expansion believed to have been initiated by the Big Bang. Divide the distance of a galaxy by the speed at which it's moving, and you get what appears to be a fairly accurate guess as to the age of the whole darned thing. Again— within five billion years or so. (Recent research has raised intriguing questions about the speed at which the universe continues to expand. Steer clear of this.)

If you want to impress in a major way, try this: "I can't wait till the next syzygy—can you?" It's pronounced *SIZZ-ih-jee,* and it's an alignment of three celestial objects. If you've ever seen an eclipse, you've witnessed a syzygy. (The three celestial objects, of course, would be the earth, the moon, and the sun.) Great word to pop into the conversation when things are a little dull, don't you think? My theory is that scientists come up with words like this and googolplex just to see if they can get non-scientists to say them in public.

When You Want to Change the Subject...

...point out that all those immense spans of time and space put questions of, say, mid-life crisis or interpersonal conflict into their true perspective. What's to get maudlin about? We're only here for a tiny stretch of time anyway. Why not enjoy ourselves while the ride lasts? (If that's not a satisfactory prelude to a request for a martini or a decision to play *From a Distance* on the jukebox, or both, I don't know what is.)

Words to the Wise

Careful! Discussions of the solar system may require you to display your knowledge of the relative sizes of the nine planets that orbit the sun. They are, from largest to smallest, Jupiter, Saturn, Uranus, Neptune, Earth, Venus, Mars, Mercury, and Pluto. Jupiter and Saturn are in a planetary league of their own at 142,984 kilometers and 120,536 kilometers in diameter, respectively. Earth's diameter is roughly one-tenth that of Jupiter's; Pluto's diameter is a little over one-sixth that of Earth's. And, just in case someone starts pressuring you about the sun, that's 1,392,000 kilometers in diameter—nearly ten times the size of Jupiter.

The U.S. Constitution and the Supreme Court

The U.S. Constitution is the document everyone talks about—but hardly anybody bothers to read. You can find the text in any good almanac, but what's the ultimate impact of the words that come after "We, the people"? Here's the lowdown on where this remarkable political document came from, what it actually means, and how it's been interpreted over the centuries.

The Straight Scoop

To understand the origin of the Constitution, it helps to understand the (extremely tenuous) means by which the rebelling American states had united to oppose British domination during the War of Independence. You might even say that the former colonies never truly established *any* effective national authority during this period; instead, by means of the Articles of Confederation (1781) they delegated to "this confederacy" only the powers that they could not themselves undertake—reserving, for instance, the power to levy taxes to the individual states. The pragmatic grouping that initially prevailed, known as the The "United States of America in Congress Assembled," is best understood as a gathering of governments with certain mutual interests, rather than as a single nation with an acknowledged sovereignty. A glimpse of the status of the central government in the pre-Constitutional period can be seen in the fact that Canada was invited—but declined—to join the United States. That term was, significantly, always regarded as a plural noun ("The United States are ...")—a practice that persisted until after the American Civil War.

After victory against the British was achieved, the shortcomings of the federal union's structure were the topic of much discussion. The Continental Congress declined to take a leading role in any reformulation, choosing instead to leave the matter to state legislatures. A number of representatives of individual states gathered at Annapolis in 1786 to examine the possibility of strengthening the federal authority; one of those present, Alexander Hamilton—a long-time supporter of the idea of a more powerful national government—proposed that representatives of all the states meet in Philadelphia in May, 1787 "to render the Constitution of the Federal government adequate to the exigencies of the union." Congress voted in favor of Hamilton's plan; Hamilton himself served as a delegate at that convention, which was attended by delegates from every state except Rhode Island.

The new Constitution was drafted in 1787, ratified in 1788, and declared to be in effect on March 4, 1789. (Eventually, all thirteen of the former colonies ratified the Constitution.) So—what had been ratified? What, precisely, did the delegates who attended the Constitutional Convention accomplish? They hammered out a flexible, compromise-heavy, and often deliberately vague document that, in its seven articles, laid down the fundamental law of the United States and formulated a central federal authority. That central government, if not as powerful as Hamilton might have preferred, nevertheless boasted significant powers that dwarfed those of the anemic structure it replaced. This new central authority was divided into three separate branches: legislative (Congress), executive (the president), and judicial (the courts). The central government's new powers were carefully apportioned between the three branches, which were meant to act as checks upon one another. As though to emphasize the open-ended nature of the relatively brief document, the Constitution also provided the means for its own revision—amendments, which must be ratified by three-quarters of all the states of the union.

It didn't take long for important amendments to pop up. To limit the power of the central government, ten amendments to the Constitution were ratified (1791). Popularly known as the Bill of Rights, these amendments protected: religious freedom, freedom of the press, the right of peaceable assembly, and the right to petition the government (Amendment I); the right to keep and bear arms (Amendment II); rights of citizens not to have their homes turned into military quarters without their consent (Amendment III); rights against unreasonable search and seizure (Amendment IV); rights against overzealous prosecution and appropriation of life, liberty, or property without due process of law (Amendment V); rights to a speedy trial and to legal counsel (Amendment VI); rights of trial by jury (Amendment VII); freedom from excessive bail, fines, and cruel and unusual punishment; and the retention of rights by the people, and powers by the states (Amendments IX and X).

But wait! You get more than just ten amendments! As the country grew, others were ratified. Among the most important: Amendments XIII, XIV, and XV, which abolished slavery, guaranteed citizenship rights without abridgment, and rejected race as a barrier to voting rights; Amendment XVI, which established the federal authority to tax personal incomes (that's the IRS, friends—an institution I, like so many other Americans, have always feared and loathed); Amendments XVIII and XXII, which instituted (1919) and repealed (1933), respectively, prohibition against the sale of liquor; and Amendment XIX, which extended the right to vote to women.

What You Can Say

When discussing the Constitution, you're well advised to have at least a summary knowledge of four or five of the most crucial Supreme Court cases that have come down over the centuries. What follows are intelligent remarks on some of the real blockbuster decisions.

"People sometimes forget that there's nothing in the Constitution itself that designates the Supreme Court as the final interpreter of constitutional disputes. That role only emerged in *Marbury v.*

Madison." (This all-important 1803 case, the foundation of all authoritative constitutional review by the judiciary, established the Supreme Court's power to examine acts of Congress—and to invalidate those deemed unconstitutional.)

"The final remedy for excesses or errors on the part of the Court, of course, is the Constitutional amendment. When a case like *Dred Scott v. Sanford* comes along, we have to compensate with something like the fourteenth Amendment." (The Dred Scott case is usually preceded by the adjective "infamous" in written accounts of the Court's history. The decision overturned the Missouri Compromise, which had already been repealed, on the logic that Congress had deprived slaveowners of their property—slaves—without due process of law. The Scott case was also the occasion of the Court's explicit ruling that slaves were not citizens of the United States or of any individual state. The fourteenth Amendment, ratified in 1868, declared all persons born or naturalized in the United States to be "citizens of the United States and of the state wherein they reside.")

"It took *Gitlow v. New York* to force state governments to hold themselves accountable to the Bill of Rights." (The landmark 1925 case was the first of a number to hold that the 14th Amendment mandated compliance with the Bill of Rights by the individual states. In this case, the issue was state interference with freedom of speech.)

"As momentous as *Brown vs. Board of Education* was, you have to remember that it was limited to situations where explicit, formal action from the government resulted in separate and unequal facilities." (The breakthrough 1954 case, which focused only on the calculated *de jure* discriminatory policies of state and local authorities, established that the unequal treatment of schoolchildren was in direct violation of the equal protection clause of the fourteenth Amendment. It left unaddressed questions of *de facto* segregation—discrimination arising from trends unprompted by government policy.)

"Sometimes the Court hands down decisions that seem to be pointing in two directions at once. The *Bakke* case is probably the most famous recent example of this." (The high-profile 1978 case *Regents of the University of California v. Bakke* ruled both that the university's practice of setting aside a predetermined number of places for minorities was in violation of law, *and* that admissions programs using race as one of a number of factors in considering student applications for admission was constitutional.)

When You Want to Change the Subject...

...you can always put the emphasis on the flexibility and resiliency of the constitutional system—and steer your way clear of scholarly waters you don't feel like navigating. Use a remark like the following:

"Well, if the country can make it through a crisis like *U.S. v. Nixon*, it can probably make it through anything." (In this 1974 case, undertaken with extraordinary speed and delivered in a unanimous ruling, the Supreme Court held that claims of absolute executive privilege against the demands of the judiciary for evidence relevant to a criminal trial were unjustified. The Nixon administration had argued that the principle of separation of constitutional powers, and the need for maintaining confidentiality in presidential communications, justified such protection. Disputes over the evidence in the Nixon case led to one of the most daunting constitutional crises in the nation's history. Nixon's resignation in the face of almost certain conviction during Senate impeachment proceedings is often cited as evidence that the system—that is to say, the constitutional system— works.)

Words to the Wise

Over the years, interpreting the Constitution has emerged as a cyclical, and long-lasting, pursuit. Even seemingly definitive decisions have given rise to new interpretations and new rulings; even minority dissents have served, decades later, as the basis for important new principles.

As time has passed, two primary approaches have battled for predominance when it comes to saying what, precisely, the Constitution means. One strategy, exemplified by Earl Warren (chief justice, 1953–1969) has come to be known as the broad construction or judicial activism school. This school has been associated with the idea that the contemporary values of the society, when combined with the values of individual justices, may play a legitimate role in determining the overall direction of the judiciary's decisions. The opposing school, known as the strict construction or judicial restraint school, argues that courts in general, and the Supreme Court in particular, should be bound by the words and intentions of the original framers of the Constitution.

Any discussion with a person knowledgeable about constitutional law is likely to lead to a discussion of these two approaches; you'll probably be expected to have an opinion as to the relative merits of both schools of thought. The easiest (and, providentially, most accurate) response in this area is simply to say that the Constitution needs both approaches, and that each should be expected to experience periods of dominance and decline.

HOW TO IMPRESS ANYBODY ABOUT

Zen Buddhism

This book closes with what may be the trickiest entry of them all. Writing about Zen Buddhism is a little more problematic than writing about most other forms of organized religion, in that Zen rejects analytical efforts to understand the divine, and sees interpretive language (for instance, the words I'm typing now on my little computer) as a barrier to the direct, open experience of life. So why write about it at all? Well, it seems the more Zen rejects verbal descriptions of itself, the more people seem to be attracted to it. And you may just run into someone who feels like chatting about this extremely influental branch of Buddhism.

Herewith a few more words to add to the already massive mountain of texts about this essentially text-averse religious tradition. You can either read them—or, if you're feeling particularly ambitious, toss them into the fire.

The Straight Scoop

Zen is a sect of Buddhism that is said to have arisen in China around the fifth century A.D.; it can be traced from China to Japan, where its emphasis on prolonged periods of meditation, direct personal experience of reality, and full attentiveness during all daily activities was a big hit. Over the centuries, Zen thrived in Japan and had a major cultural impact in areas such as calligraphy and the martial arts. But far more important than its cultural impact was its ongoing sense of personal commitment to individual authenticity and complete presence—no matter what.

The very word Zen is derived from a Sanskrit word for meditation, and that's what serious Zen practitioners do: meditate. They view scriptures, long-winded technical discourses, and a heavy emphasis on formal dogma as potentially dangerous, and as a result they rely heavily on tools that are regarded as likely to be of help in transcending mental delusions and discovering one's Buddha-nature. Such tools may include not only meditation, but the famous *koans*— paradoxical queries (like "What is the sound of one hand clapping?") that are meant to help strip away inauthentic, second-hand conclusions. Practitioners generally study under the guidance of a master, whose job it is to help the student strip away veils and attain true self-realization.

Important figures in the history of Zen include the Third Patriarch, Seng-ts'an, under whom Zen embraced many aspects of Taoism (which reveres the processes of nature), and the Sixth Patriarch, Hui-Neng, who focused intently on the discovery (or is that rediscovery?) of one's original mind and true nature.

What You Can Say

Whatever you do, keep it simple. You might choose to say something like the following: "As I understand it, the main point is to promote 100 percent engagement, without distraction, in whatever one is doing, whether that's formal sitting meditation, or everyday activity. Like talking to you."

When You Want to Change the Subject...

...just change the subject.

Words to the Wise

The wise don't need many words.